THERE'S NOTHING OUT THERE

Black Shuck Books
www.blackshuckbooks.co.uk

First published in Great Britain in 2025 by
Black Shuck Books
Kent, UK

All essays © their respective authors 2025

Set in Caslon
Cover & interior design © WHITEspace, 2025
www.white-space.uk

The rights of the author of this work have been asserted by them in accordance with the Copyright, Designs and Patents Act, 1988.
All rights reserved. No part of this publication may be reproduced or transmitted in any form or by any means, electronic or mechanical, including photocopy, recording, or any information storage and retrieval system, without permission in writing from the publisher.
This book is a work of fiction. Names, characters, businesses, organisations, places and events are either the product of the author's imagination or are used fictitiously. Any resemblance to actual persons, living or dead, events or locales is entirely coincidental.

978-1-917173-06-3

There's Nothing Out There

edited by

Sophie Essex

Contents

* * *

Introduction . . . . *vii*

Lost in the Middle of Nowhere: The Rules of Survival
    Jason Gould 11

Swiss Army Man and the Big Two-Hearted River Tradition
    Pete W Sutton 23

To Live in Fear… or Not?
    Darcy L Wood 31

'Have a drink, mate?': Alcoholism, Social Anxiety and Loss of Identity in *Wake in Fright*
    Dan Coxon 39

Always Staring Into Dark Corners
    Gaynor Jones 49

Get Lost, Spider-Man!
    Daragh Fleming 57

Ozploitation, HBO, Unfettered Ferocity and *Fortress*
    Adam Groves 65

The Use of the Supernatural in *Long Weekend*
    Marcelle Perks 73

Event Horizon
    Benjamin Kurt Unsworth 83

Navigating Out of the Backwoods: Mapping American
Lost-in-the-Wilderness Horror's Evolution and
Reconceptualising its Future
   Alex Ringer 93

Ravenous: Deus Absconditus
   Lisa Moore-Smith 109

All Sinners Are Lost: The Art of Being Lost in *As Above, So Below*
   Sarah R New 119

Into the Wild: Losing Your Life by Choice
   Frank Schildiner 125

Walkabout: The Land of Lost Content
   Gary Couzens 133

Brightwood: You Can't Go Home Again
   John G Austin 141

Fear and Loathing in the Arctic
   Andrew Hook 149

Life is a Horror Movie: The Footnotes
   Ashley Stokes 157

Recommended Viewing 179

Introduction

What's Your Favourite Scary Movie?

by Sophie Essex

It's another sunlit day in the summer of my childhood and as I scan the surrounding playground I can't see my mother; my aunt and cousins are also out of sight. I've been abandoned! At least, with the hindsight that adulthood brings, that's how it felt and how it feels still.

I despise being lost, fear of abandonment consumes me. It underpins my life in ways that exhaust me and limit my experience with the world, and so perhaps a means of processing this is via film with the heady adrenaline-fuelled thrill that survival horror provides, all from the comfort and safety of home.

I was too young to get caught up in the hype of the *The Blair Witch Project* on its initial release, but it has since become a favourite, an obsession. It's my go-to comfort film having seen it countless times, and a film I will defend at every given opportunity.

What I love most is Heather's innocent foolishness. She hopes, plots even, to lose herself, along with Josh and Mike, in the supposedly haunted woods of Maryland, for a short time knowing she has the safety of her map to find their way home... until she doesn't. I know how this ends, it's 'standard horror movie stuff', terrifying on every single rewatch, and I love it. Another reason why I wanted to edit this anthology of similar themes.

It was Jean-Luc Godard that said *It's not where you take things from, it's where you take them to* and so the title of this anthology is borrowed from the 1991 comedy horror film of the same name, directed by Rolfe Kanefsky. Considered the first self-referential meta horror, this low-budget flick provides a wealth of inspiration for the horror fan, as well as a great title. It's a blueprint for *Scream* (1996, Wes Craven), which draws heavily – too heavily, maybe – from *There's Nothing Out There*.

If you can, watch the short documentary film, *Copycat* (2015, Charlie Shackleton), which expands on this. Inevitably, of course, much horror *is* derivative, especially so, perhaps, with survival horror.

But that is also why I love it and why I wanted to share this love with others. And of course, an anthology of essays and passion pieces was the perfect vessel. I am forever honoured when people trust me with their work, especially when writers share their vulnerabilities; such as Dan Coxon's piece on his struggle with alcoholism whilst living in an unfamiliar country and how he saw this mirrored in *Wake In Fright*, or Ashley Stokes coming to terms with his mother's passing, or how Gaynor Jones also found within *The Blair Witch Project* an echo of her fears.

You'll find the expected here: *The Texas Chain Saw Massacre*, *Walkabout*, *The Descent*; but also the unexpected: *Spider-Man*, *Into The Wild*, *Swiss Army Man*; as well as the lesser known: *Arctic Void*, *Fortress*. I was excited by how each writer expanded on the theme of loss and took it to a new direction, especially as there is a parallel to be found in the editing process. I had to abandon myself and my idea to others, lose myself for a while, anxiety building, until I found myself questioning if the process would ever end, speculating on where the path forged by the contributors might lead, until finally everything comes together and I realise that as an editor I've not been abandoned yet.

I hope you appreciate the enthusiasm these writers have for their chosen works. But reader beware: there's nothing out there, except, inevitably, a few spoilers.

Lost in the Middle of Nowhere

The Rules of Survival

by Jason Gould

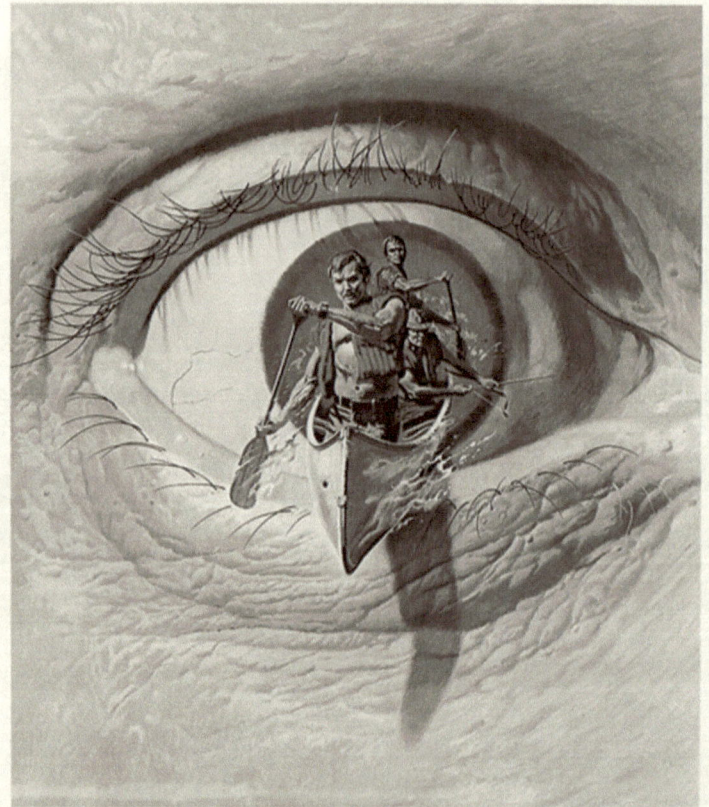

In meta-slasher *Scream* (1996) film geek Randy claims that the only way to survive in a horror movie, and avoid being the next victim, is to follow a set of predefined rules:

"Rule #1: Never have sex."
"Rule #2: Never drink or do drugs."
"Rule #3: Never ever, under any circumstances, say 'I'll be right back' – because you won't be."

Defining the rules of the slasher movie, within a slasher movie, provided free reign for director Wes Craven to bend and break those rules, and have good fun at the same time. However, it only worked due to the sizeable canon of films that had accumulated in the slasher genre since its earliest days. Popular classics such as *Psycho* (1960), *Halloween* (1978), and *Friday the 13th* (1980) embedded their narrative style deep within our collective memory, and furnished the audience with the necessary cultural reference points – rules that movie fans had previously known but failed to consciously acknowledge – to appreciate the point Craven was attempting to make. Familiarity, it seems, breeds pastiche – not that *Scream* is a pastiche, more an exercise in meta-storytelling.

Films in which the principle characters become hopelessly lost and steeped in peril have increased in recent years and amassed a similar oeuvre. Like the slasher genre, or any genre populated enough to establish an identifiable pattern, it is possible to step back, observe, and define the rules…

Rule #1: Never accept an invitation to visit an idyllic rural landscape… for it will surely be populated by local folk keen to protect their unique way of life from meddling outsiders

"At the edge of a great forest…" So begins the cautionary tale of *Hansel and Gretel*, in which the titular characters find themselves abandoned in the darkest part of the forest by their own mother and father as they were unable to afford to feed them. The Brothers Grimm were writing in the early 19th century, in Germany, but foregoing the security of home by stepping into an unfamiliar, dangerous landscape applies equally to modern day films, especially those in which the characters end up lost in the back of beyond and confronted by people with whom they are simply never going to see eye to eye.

Deliverance (1972) is perhaps the most well-known film that lifts city slickers out of their comfort zone and deposits them in an environment which feels like another world, not just geographically, but socially and culturally. It follows the story of four businessmen (Lewis, Ed, Bobby, Drew) on a canoe expedition down the Cahulawassee river (in real life the Chattooga River, Georgia) – a trip that turns out to be less back-to-nature than back-to-survival. Like Hansel and Gretel, the group fall prey to the dark threat at the centre of the forest, not an evil witch – as befell the children – but a pair of Grizzly Adams-types (albeit less cuddly and far less wholesome than Adams) who orchestrate a pointless argument about the river, and whiskey, as a ruse to spark the conflict that sets the trajectory for the rest of the film. Events escalate, including the rape of Bobby at gunpoint, during which he is forced to engage in the kind of dirty talk reserved for such special occasions in these here parts (the infamous "squeal piggy squeal" dialogue). The city-types escape and a game of cat and mouse ensues, through the forest and along the river; the good old boys, representing the old guard, versus the suburbanites, representing an unwelcome force for change – all of which is mirrored in a subtle piece of symbolism: the violent change due to be forced upon the natural world by the building of a dam. Sadly, however, it is not the unstoppable march of civilisation for which many remember *Deliverance*; it is remembered more for its portrayal of backwoods America – old timers in rocking chairs, duelling banjos, locals with poor dental hygiene – which would set the standard for cliché, parody, and eventually the sub-genre that is *hicksploitation*.

Symbolism is noticeably absent from many films that followed *Deliverance*. Despite a plot that unfolds at pace, and some truly horrific moments, *Rituals* (1977), for example, lacks the punch and originality of the film that was clearly its blueprint. An ill-fated group of doctors set out on a fishing trip to remote Northern Ontario. Soon, however, matters descend into *Deliverance* territory, and they are picked off one by one, stalked and murdered by a hidden-until-the-end-of-the-film assailant who turns out to be, quite randomly, a disfigured cabin-dwelling war veteran named Matthew Crowley, intent on revenge (it's hinted that said revenge is against medical professionals per se and not the human race at large, but this is not entirely obvious). Frustratingly, the juxtaposition of medicine and war is not properly explored, which feels like a missed opportunity. It would seem that the surgeons represent the people who attempted to heal Matthew Crowley of his war wounds but made matters worse; however a deeper exploration, into how medicine can cure a multitude of ailments but not those inflicted by humanity against itself, would have proved more satisfying. Lacking that extra dimension, *Rituals* is simply a film about being lost, without the additional metaphor that makes films about being lost that bit more enjoyable.

It would take the vision of a director with sensibilities usually found at the arthouse end of the spectrum to help the *Deliverance*-esque film carve its own fresh and unique niche. Obscure, odd, and deeply disturbing, *Calvaire* (2004) – known also as *The Ordeal* – occupies such a position, cleverly flipping its predecessors on their collective head.

In the French-Belgian production, travelling singer Marc Stevens breaks down far from anywhere and is taken in by friendly innkeeper, Mr. Bartel. Stevens intends to stay one night, fix his van, and move on. It would seem, however, that Bartel, lonely and desperate for company, would prefer Stevens to stay longer – a stay that he forces to happen by preventing the singer from leaving, tying him to a chair, shaving half his head, and forcing him to wear his dead wife's dress (for whom Bartel is grieving); he also attempts to crucify the object of his obsession. And it gets weirder, including a scene in the local bar where the townsfolk dance a distorted waltz, which has to be one of the most disturbing scenes ever. *Calvaire* is the wonderful magic that happens when traditional film finds itself reinvigorated creatively. It flips the lost-in-the-forest, threatened-by-locals storyline: the insular, inward-dwelling villain welcomes the stranger, and wants him to be part of his life – forever.

Films such as *Deliverance* and *Rituals* would inspire the likes of Rob Zombie's *House of 1000 Corpses* (2003) and *The Devils' Rejects*, while *Calvaire* would push forest-based isolation and conflict down an entirely different avenue, leading, perhaps, to films such as Lars Von Trier's *Antichrist* (2009).

Wherever you find yourself – old school or arthouse – always observe Rule #1. And remember, "Ain't nuthin for folks like you round here."

Rule #2: Never order from the Specials Board, unless you're partial to diced hitch-hiker marinated in moonshine and served on a bed of freshly sourced roadkill…

Later in the story of *Hansel and Gretel*, once the forest – literal and symbolic – has been entered, the children encounter a gingerbread house, where they are held captive by a witch, whose intention is to fatten up Hansel and pop him in the oven for dinner (the witch seems to have a predilection for eating little boys rather than little girls). It is the next step in the gruesome fairy-tale that warns against the twin perils of straying from the path and succumbing to sweet delights (although the children, starving and abandoned by their impoverished parents, have little choice in either matter). Similarly, it was the next step for films in which the characters end up lost, raising the threat level from being lost and in fear for their lives, to being lost, in fear for their lives, and destined for the dinner plate. Not the halcyon day trip they had planned.

A day trip, the reality of which turns out *much* different to that which was planned, forms the backdrop to classic horror film *The Texas Chain Saw Massacre* (1974). Idyllic perfection established and then shattered is described before the film has properly begun, through the opening crawl three years before George Lucas utilised the device in *Star Wars: Episode IV – A New Hope* (1977). Narrated (unlike Star Wars which is purely text), it recounts how the five youths central to the story would witness, that day, too much of the mad and macabre, and how their perfect summer afternoon drive in the countryside would become a nightmare, when (we learn over the course of the next 83 minutes) they veer off the beaten track and encounter a family of cannibals – the most memorable of which is the Ed Gein-influenced Leatherface – intent not only on despatching interlopers but hacking them up and storing them in the freezer for haute cuisine Texan-style. It is, as the introductory voice-over claims, the stuff of nightmares: grave robbing, hammer blows to the head, a female victim hung on a meat-hook, furniture fashioned from human bones, the chainsaw of the title, and the title itself. In many ways, however, the film is quite understated. It relies on little blood, much if not all the dismemberment is off-camera, and the cannibalism simmers away suggestively but refrains from being rammed down the throat (perhaps the most nauseating reference to cannibalism is the lingering shot of what appear to be sausages sizzling over a barbecue, meat products more likely to have been 'freshly prepared on the premises' than purchased shrink-wrapped at Walmart, or whatever 1970s America preferred as its supermarket of choice). And believe it or not, no one is actually eaten in the film, despite the impression left on the audience, not to mention the censors.

Another erstwhile thorn in the side of the film censors is the aforementioned Wes Craven. Long before he indulged in self-referential, meta-storytelling with *Scream*, he contributed directly to the canon of films triggered by Leatherface & Co. with *The Hills Have Eyes* (1977). Similar in plot to its Texas-based predecessor three years earlier, it portrays the plight of the Carter family, lost and stranded in the Nevada desert after a car accident, and under attack by a family (or should that be pack) of savages who decide it's time for tea. Unlike the shenanigans over in Texas, it focuses more on the concept and construct of the family unit, contrasting the similarities and differences between the civilised Carter family, forced into primitive behaviour to protect themselves, and the feral desert-dwellers desperate to put food on the table, including the Carter's baby, snatched for the cooking pot – an interesting inclusion, since Craven claimed he wanted to be less controversial after the notoriety that surrounded *The Last House on the Left* (1972). Essentially, both families want what is right for them: survival through whatever means possible, whether that's acceptance of a kill or be killed situation, and the descent into murder, or living in the desert caves and foothills and subsisting on lost tourists. Different strokes for different folks. And, after all, values bond a family together, forever.

Even in later films that explore off-grid events, such as *Wrong Turn* (2003), the principle of family persists, no matter how odd, perverse, or inbred. Like Leatherface's kin (aside from Grandma, who's dead in the attic) the anthropophagous folk in *Wrong Turn* are all male: mountain men from a family tree with far too many interlinked branches, and whose lineage is evident in their names: Three Finger, Saw Tooth, One Eye. Comedic names, perhaps, for a film that feels quite kitsch compared to its 1970s counterparts. It's brutal and gory, without a doubt, but the mountain men shuffle and shamble about like the Honey Monster dressed in denim dungarees. (For younger readers, the Honey Monster was an oversized, yellow, furry, bug-eyed, grinning creature that walked like Frankenstein and spoke like a caveman, and was used to sell breakfast cereal on 1970s UK television, alongside Benny Hill's sidekick, Henry McGee, who, for some unknown reason, Honey Monster believed was his Mummy – yes, the 1970s was a strange time.) Perhaps *Wrong Turn* was an attempt to Hollywood-ise the helplessly-lost-and-captured-by-cannibals sub-genre. Consequently, it lacks the nasty realism that the earlier films evoke to produce the 'this is really happening' atmosphere.

But, of course, *The Texas Chain Saw Massacre* really *did* happen, according to the narrator at the outset. Could it happen again? Best not risk finding out. Obey Rule #2 and avoid putting yourself or anyone else on the end of that fork.

Rule #3: Never take your mobile phone on a trip to the wilderness, for it will be found years later containing shaky footage of your final moments...

Like many tales by the Brothers Grimm, the tale of Hansel and Gretel is all the more frightening for its authentic ring of truth. It taps into the part of the psyche that (mis)interprets the story not as fiction, but historical fact – and the belief that this is fact, and not fiction, is the scariest fact of all.

Home movies might be used to similar effect. They, of course, depict true events (most of the time). And they evoke a sense of the sinister in their own right. Why is that? Why do old home movies feel somehow not quite right, as if something is lurking beneath the surface, or just off-screen? Perhaps it's the invasion into the personal space, the forbidden glimpse behind closed doors and drawn curtains, places hidden from view for hundreds of years until the portable cine-camera found itself in the hands of the general public in the 1950s and 60s. Footage of The Beatles mobbed at airports and nude hippies freaking out at Woodstock have become long established in our collective cultural memory, mingled with childhood birthday parties, forgotten relatives at weddings, the splash of a swimming pool in a holiday camp – all caught on flickering, grainy film that, unless preserved, would fade from view.

But somewhere in that collective cultural memory bank lurks the origin of the psychological fear inherent in the found footage horror movie, the link between a few idyllic frames captured at a family picnic in the dim, distant past, and the chaos and terror unfolding on screen. Watching found footage horror movies is like watching the film-making efforts of parents and grandparents fiddling about with new technology back in the day (or for those young enough to have parents and grandparents born in the digital age, perhaps some kind of inherited memory passed down genetically from generation to generation). It's personal, as if we're watching someone's home video footage. Maybe even our own.

In a way, the first found footage horror movie was made by Abraham Zapruder. If that name fails to strike a chord among cinephiles it's because Zapruder was not a film director; he was a clothing manufacturer, who happened to be filming U.S. President John F. Kennedy's motorcade in Texas on November 22nd 1963, when a bullet, or bullets, fired by Lee Harvey Oswald (or other assassin or assassins, depending what you believe) created what would become a macabre and chilling 20th century home movie legend. Accidentally,

Zapruder captured a moment more horrific than most of the horror movies set to emerge in the next half century, for the simple fact that the events committed to film were as real as the pieces of Kennedy's skull wife Jacqueline frantically attempts to retrieve from the rear of the presidential limousine in frame 371. Like found footage films, the viewer observes that which was not meant to be observed, events that should have stayed unseen, whether it's the murder of a president or a supernatural presence attacking a victim in a cabin in the woods. And because curiosity is in our nature, and it looks and feels real, just like our own home movies, it's impossible to look away.

Shaky handheld cinematography, commentary spoken direct to the audience like a personal diary, and a script the primary purpose of which is to sound unscripted – all these parts combine to transform what is often a simple storyline into a study in abject terror. In *The Blair Witch Project*, for example, a group of students film a documentary about the legend of the Blair Witch, a supernatural entity thought to haunt the forest in which the crew decide to film (and become lost in the process) and which might or might not have been responsible for various historic murders. It was not the plot that made the film the box office smash it became, it was the close-up shots of the person holding the camera, breathing heavily, not knowing which way to run, their fear palpable, intercut with footage of the forest-floor and the night sky and perhaps the occasional glimpse of something not of this world; and, of course, the idea that the footage was lost and then later found, suggesting that the audience is watching the final hours in the lives of these hapless students.

In a brilliant move by director Fabien Delage, however, the footage in *Cold Ground* (2017) is even more authentic. Set in 1976, it follows a pair of journalists who travel to the French / Swiss border to investigate cattle mutilation, but end up hiking deep into the mountains in search of the team of scientists they were supposed to meet. They become irredeemably lost and confronted by the monster(s) behind the original mutilation. While the story and monster(s) are scary enough, it is the smart use of retro-techniques that makes *Cold Ground* deeply unsettling: scratchy, degraded film stock, crackle on the soundtrack, unsophisticated camerawork, and an atmosphere that – to borrow from philosopher Jacques Derrida – feels genuinely hauntological, as if the past is recurring, intruding on the present, and that we have been here before. And, of course, we have, in those home movies, and in the 1970s horror movies to which *Cold Ground* is paying more than a passing nod.

It's no coincidence that Delage sets *Cold Ground* in the mid-1970s. It is perhaps a deliberate homage to the film often cited (incorrectly, others preceded it, though they may not be as effective) as the first to employ found footage: *Cannibal Holocaust* (1980). Banned in multiple countries, the stomach-churning video nasty, directed by Ruggero Deodato, is part standard film-making, part found footage. The film follows a rescue mission to the Amazon rainforest, where a film crew vanished while shooting a documentary on cannibal tribes, and where their remains – and film reels – are subsequently found – reels which turn out to be footage of their final moments at the hands of the tribe. It was not just the gore that ensured the film was banned, it was the realism generated by the found footage technique; a technique that, in 1980, was relatively unknown. Its impact – the way that the recovered footage felt like a news report rather than cinema – was too much, to the point that Deodato was arrested on suspicion he'd actually had actors killed on camera (he was released when the actors proved they were alive and well). Too much realism, it seems, is too much to take, certainly back in 1980.

Nowadays, however, we can't get enough of it, through the omnipresence of digital screens, social media, and reality television. And while it might be nice to enjoy your fifteen minutes of fame, take note of the third and final rule, and make sure those fifteen minutes are not your last.

It's no surprise that most characters in the films listed fail to heed the warnings. Why would they? If they did, each film would be brief and boring: everyone would be suitably kitted out with map and compass, the weather would not turn, no one would break their ankle – and, of course, the locals would welcome the visitors with open arms, only too glad to go out of their way to make their holiday comfortable and restful. But where's the fun in that?

It would appear that an additional rule is required, if it's not just about survival, but fun. And that rule is: ignore rules #1, #2, and #3. If you dare.

Swiss Army Man
and the Big Two-Hearted River Tradition
by Pete W Sutton

In chapter 8 of *Into the Wild* by John Krakauer, a book about being lost in the wilderness – sort of lost, deliberately lost – there's an epigraph:

"We have in America 'The Big Two-Hearted River' tradition: taking your wounds to the wilderness for a cure, a conversion, a rest, or whatever."

—Edward Hoagland - *Up the Black to Chalkyttsik*

Hoagland's piece is itself an essay about a river trip in the wilderness of Alaska. *Into the Wild* (itself now a film) was very much on my mind when I rewatched *Swiss Army Man*, directed by Daniels' Scheinert and Kwan, and starring Paul Dano, Daniel Radcliffe (as a farting corpse) and Mary Elizabeth Winstead. It may not be set in Alaska (rather, filmed in Humboldt county California – of giant redwood fame) but is very much in this tradition.

The Daniels may now be instantly recognisable due to *Everything Everywhere All at Once*, which swept the awards in 2022, but I came to them through music and was very much looking forward to *Swiss Army Man*, their debut feature film, and was not disappointed. Back in 2011 when we still watched MTV – or at least had it on in the background while doing other stuff – the Daniels directed a music video for Manchester Orchestra's single *Simple Math* which included a slow-motion car crash with the band inside the car. Their visual style was immediately striking and I watched a few of their other videos and therefore went to see *Swiss Army Man* on release in 2016.

Swiss Army Man is a film about a man lost in the wilderness who befriends a corpse, and together they have adventures while striving to return to civilisation. At the beginning of the film, we see a series of increasingly desperate notes written on floating trash which serve as the film's opening exposition. "I was on a boat and got lost in a storm," one reads. "I just want to go home and start over," says another and "stranded: send help," several state. The final one says "Nevermind (sic). I'm dead." And we see Hank (Paul Dano) standing on a picnic ice box with a noose around his neck humming what becomes the theme tune of the film. He spots the corpse of a man – Manny (Daniel Radcliffe) – whose farts allow Hank to ride him like a jet ski back to the mainland.

"It's only funny because it's a life and death situation, with farts!" – Daniel Kwan.

The first thing Hank does when he returns to the mainland is to check his phone (on 10% battery) for a signal and we see that his save screen is a picture of Sarah (Mary Elizabeth Winstead). And so, we have our first intimation as to why Hank is lost in the wilderness. He's run away. As the film progresses, we discover that Hank feels judged as unworthy (his father often calls him retarded) and takes himself too seriously. This is shown, physically, in Hank's inability to fart around Manny. And it is this wound, this lack of understanding of the absurdity of life, that needs to be healed. He's escaped, but is having second thoughts: "I just want to go home and start over."

The music for the film was composed by Andy Hull and Robert McDowell of Manchester Orchestra after being sent the script by the Daniels with the intention that the band would write a song for the film. Hull decided he wanted to score it – a first for him, having never scored a film before – and he roped in McDowell to help. The Daniels specified that the music had to be created without instruments, only using singing and 'body sounds'. Thankfully it turned out better than Roger Waters' *Music from the Body* album!

Since the music was mostly written before the film, Hull was able to integrate it into the performances of Dano & Radcliffe from the start, and therefore the score forms an integral part of the film. They also asked John Williams for permission to have a purely vocal version of the *Jurassic Park* theme tune, which he graciously allowed as long as the film wasn't a porno. In general, the music is uplifting. It's worth listening to – and watching the video for – 'Montage' from the soundtrack.

"The whole film is about loneliness and the shame that keeps you from love."

– Daniel Scheinert.

The film starts with trash which is used as a motif throughout. Hank builds a bus out of sticks and trash, he shows Manny (once Manny has 'come alive') shadow puppet versions of popular films, like *Jurassic Park*, and he mostly – until Manny's powers fully manifest and Hank is able to hunt and fish – takes his nourishment from food that people have thrown away; including in one joyful sequence when they finally have fire – popcorn!

Very much the – not so subtle – subliminal message is that Hank has been discarded from society – he's literally trash. Manny is a corpse that isn't claimed who, once he comes alive, asks:

MANNY – Where are all the dead people? Do they hide them?
HANK – Yeah.
MANNY – So I'm like trash?

Manny never stops being a corpse but he becomes a useful box of tricks on top of his fart power – he can produce drinking water from his mouth, shoot things with objects placed *in* his mouth, karate chop things in half, and produce sparks from his fingers. He's a Swiss Army Man. Hank assists Manny in his quest to remember the world, and in doing so Hank remembers all the good stuff *he's* missing. Another of Manny's functions is that when he gets an erection (from looking at swimwear models), his penis points the way home. Hank utilises this by lying to Manny, telling him that Sarah is his own girlfriend, whereby Manny's sexual attraction to the picture of her on Hank's phone becomes the compass that will take them home. And so, Hank sets off to return to civilisation.

Hemingway's 'Big Two-Hearted River' is one of his Nick Adams stories in which Adams, wounded in WW1, takes himself off to fish for trout in Montana. It was the first of Hemingway's 'Iceberg' stories and the healing is very much for mental, rather than physical wounds. The USA, like Australia and New Zealand, has enough wilderness remaining for people to 'go bush'. After contemplating the river and the trout, Adams is reinvigorated and hopeful. He sees that the river is unchanging and the destruction of the war must end at some point. Nature is regenerative and perpetual. He is 'healed' by his encounter with the wilderness.

Like Chris McCandless in *Into the Wild*, people are commonly drawn into the wilderness to eschew civilisation; the natural conclusion being that modern society makes us sick and only prolonged retreats in nature can cure us of this ailment. Spending time in nature can have a healing effect on mental and physical health. For example, the Japanese have a therapeutic practice, Shinrin-yoku (forest bathing), that involves spending time in a forest to relax and de-stress.

The greater the depth of civilisation-illness, the further from society it seems people want to get. Throw in macho culture, the 'I can live off the land by hunting and fishing and other manly pursuits', and man's (used here to mean mankind, but a lot of these explorer/hermit types *are* men after all) propensity to escape, and you end up with people ill-suited to living in the wild and becoming lost.

The need for physically healing from the ills of civilisation was explored in the TV show *Northern Exposure*, also interestingly set in Alaska, with the character Mike Monroe – a hyperallergic lawyer who comes to Cicely to live in a physical bubble like *Bubble Boy* (the John Travolta film and its remake starring Jake Gyllenhaal). Monroe is literally sick of civilisation – in one episode he has a flare of psoriasis due to oil fires hundreds of miles away. Monroe, eventually, is re-integrated due to Cicely being a society of adventurous misfits to which people flee, healing them of their mental and physical ailments. The sickness inherent in modern civilisation is narratively embodied, metaphor made physical.

However, in *Swiss Army Man*, the illness is very much mental. And throughout, the viewer is never sure if Manny is just an imaginary friend. The denouement can be read as part of Hank's psychosis, in which Hank returns to society, finds it still dysfunctional and himself unwanted, and Manny leaves to return to the wilderness. This is despite the people around Hank – Sarah, his father, the TV crew, the police – all bearing witness to Manny's final use of his first, and greatest, power of farting. However Hank, in letting out his own fart to show Manny he's learned the lesson, demonstrates that he is no longer overwhelmed by how he is judged by others. He is healed of the shame that keeps you from love and ready to re-embrace society. Even if Sarah is unavailable, he has learned, through Manny, the true power of friendship.

Sarah is, for Hank, an unobtainable fantasy girlfriend – someone who has her own life, a husband and a child, and is probably unaware of Hank except for that one time she smiled at him on the bus.

SARAH – This is your phone? Why am I on your phone?
HANK – I'm sorry. You seemed really… nice. I thought maybe one day I'd get the courage to talk to you.
SARAH – What the fuck.

Of course, no trip into the wilderness is safe from the dangers of the wild. This is part of the healing process too. Modern life with its deadlines and stress – commuting on the bus (an oft-returned to motif in the film), hustling for a raise or a promotion, interacting with strangers, running out of phone battery – is full of pseudo dangers that an encounter with real danger will cure you from thinking too much about, thereby letting the lizard mind cope with a truly existence-threatening situation rather than mis-react to existential angst.

The dangers of the wild are metaphorically embodied in a bear which, in the most gruesome scene of the film, attacks Hank and badly wounds him before Manny comes to the rescue. This is a reminder to viewers that nature is red in tooth and claw and although may cure your ills, it may also kill you. Something to consider alongside all those modern gurus who profess that in order to ground oneself, one needs to spend time in nature. Mount Snowdon, for example, now referred to as Yr Wyddfa, may be a semi-domesticated piece of wilderness that seemingly requires little in the way of mountain-climbing nous, but there were over three hundred Mountain Rescue callouts last year. Seeking the healing power of nature comes with risks.

The dichotomy between doing and being, the yin and yang of living, comes to the fore as Hank and Manny try to return home – a central tenet of the film being 'don't think, just be'. This comes to a head when they are confronted by the bear, and Hank uses Manny's fart power to propel them into a tree. Manny has just discovered that Sarah is not his girlfriend and is undergoing 'baby's first existential crisis' (as the script has it.)

HANK – Manny, whatever you are doing, please stop.
MANNY – (dazed) I'm just… thinking.
HANK – Well, stop thinking.
MANNY – I can't help it. This is a thought.

As with all good stories there is death – the real danger of it alongside the symbolic. Manny becomes inert in the tree after Hank falls out of it. He reverts to being dead, as Hank is dragged slowly away by the bear. But their last words resonate: discussing death, its absurdity, and how that very absurdity means we shouldn't fear it, means that Manny's small death here is shortened. He falls from the tree, and in his first self-made movements, he sets himself on fire and scares off the bear.

But is being dead such a bad thing? In the opening scene Hank is suicidal, but even though Manny is dead his superpowers mean he can rescue Hank. Perhaps seeking healing in the wilderness and dying isn't too bad? Except that was definitely not the lesson of *Into The Wild*. McCandless made some errors of judgement that eventually cost him his life, and the book, and film, send a clear message that this could happen to anyone. McCandless was prepared, despite it appearing that he wasn't. Or is it that *Swiss Army Man*'s message about death is that as long as someone remembers you, you're not really dead? Is it that civilisation will always make you sick, so make time to get away? Manny, as a corpse without much in the way of civilizational memory, is the perfect ingenue type character for Hank to explore the absurdity of modern living.

HANK – ...We need to concentrate on getting home.
MANNY – Okay. I'm trying to remember, what is home?

The absurdist quality of the film, and the directors' follow-up, *Everything Everywhere All at Once*, remind us how meaningless the world can be, and that even the search for meaning itself is absurd. Both films are quite nihilistic at heart, existentially so. And yet, there's a joy, a finding of personal meaning despite a moral vacuum, as the Daniels use that absurdism to get to a deeper truth.

MANNY – Maybe everyone's a little bit ugly. And maybe we're all just ugly, dying sacks of shit, and maybe all it'll take is one person to just be okay with that, and then the whole world will be dancing and singing and farting, and everyone will feel a little bit less alone.

Is it OK to feel a little bit alone, if you have an imagination? Learning to love yourself, with all the unlovable qualities we possess, is the first step in letting others love you. Retreating to the wilderness has allowed Hank to see that inanity and stop taking himself too seriously. The catharsis of being able to fart in front of other people stands in for the absurdity of the guilt and shame and taboos we place upon ourselves. We are ridiculous, but so is everyone else. And we should remember that. As Hank tells Manny, everybody poops.

To Live *In Fear*... or Not?

by Darcy L Wood

© Big Talk Productions

We've all been lost, but for those of us born with only half a sense of direction, this can be a menace. For many years I worked in event hospitality, which involved trying to find huge country piles hidden down winding lanes at dusk. More often than not, I'd get lost and struggle to get enough signal to call my manager, who was rubbish at directions but excellent for moral support. Because of those hours spent driving around rural British lanes with high hedgerows and scant passing places, the horror film that speaks to me on a deeper level is *In Fear*.

The year 2013 was memorable for the horsemeat scandal, the deaths of Nelson Mandela and Margaret Thatcher, and the first time most of us set eyes on Nigel Farage's ugly mug as UKIP unexpectedly won local elections, which all seems somehow prescient today. *Frozen* was the top-grossing film and hot on its heels was Marvel's *Iron Man 3*, while *12 Years a Slave* received three Oscars and was undoubtedly the most critically acclaimed. In horror, there were unsettling originals such as *Willow Creek* (Bigfoot, found footage scares) and questionable remakes including *Evil Dead* and *Carrie*. Perhaps that's why *In Fear* stands out? It's an outlier, not being American, found footage or a sequel.

Tom (Iain De Caestecker) invites Lucy (Alice Englert) to a music festival in Ireland, even though they've only known each other for a couple of weeks. After driving from the ferry in his old Vauxhall, the young couple stop at a pub populated by unfriendly locals before setting off for the festival. However, Tom has a surprise for Lucy. He has booked one night at the fancy-looking Kilairney House Hotel. Somone in a car is supposed to show up and lead the way to the place, which they do, shortly before buggering off. Tom and Lucy let themselves in through a shut farm gate in the middle of nowhere and get royally lost. When the sun goes down it becomes clear that someone is changing signs around, and not in a puckish *Labyrinth* (1986) kind of way. It's a tried and tested premise that's oh so effective.

The whole plot is encapsulated in the opening scene. Lucy is on the toilet at the pub, reading graffiti. Unbeknownst to her, she's being watched through a hole in the cubicle wall as she adds a sarcastic 'or not' to a confusing passage that reads like a biblical proverb, about an innocent man enacting evil being the fool who will be destroyed. Perhaps it's this correction that spurs the entire plot, or is it all because a local thug bumps Tom and spills his beer? *In Fear* is a psychological horror, which means there's a third person thwarting the couple. Max (Allen Leech) is seemingly another victim of the maddening events until he's revealed later as the psychotic antagonist.

The thing horror does wonderfully is place characters in horrible situations that reveal their true selves. We as the audience love to think we'd act differently, be the hero perhaps, but horror reveals another primal fear. What if we do resort to being that scared and emotional person who acts stupidly? Tom is a fabulous example of this. When the turd hits the fan, he crumbles. His character works on naïve optimism, then denial, before drowning his fear in alcohol and getting snappy until he breaks down. There's a tiny part of me that wanted Tom to suffer because he's revealed as a wimp, but a bigger part of me felt outraged that he's bullied by Max. In a fit of rage, there's a scene where Tom nearly beats Max up, but he fails even at that. This taps into our own fears about what we might do when it comes to hard situations. Tom is the ultimate victim.

Lucy is not a victim. She is strong and wants to fight. When their predicament is revealed, Lucy is the one willing to face danger. She is the one you root for, and although she makes mistakes, at least she tries. The couple's gender roles have been flipped; the woman has oodles of pluck, whereas the man is consumed by fear, rendering him incompetent. That doesn't stop Lucy being the one grabbed and tormented, but she isn't the one who ultimately breaks.

Max is an instigator, a bully and a psychopath with a death wish. His motivation is to watch the couple suffer. He wants to scare them and feeds off their negative emotions, which ultimately leads to his demise. He is a modern-day Iago, plotting horrible things against the couple without solid motivation.

Cinematography is where this film excels. From the get-go we are introduced to frenetic, claustrophobic camera work as masterful as the chiaroscuro lighting and restricted shots of film noir, but much less stable. This is wilder, using any opportunity for the environment to obscure shots. When it's dark, we follow the two headlights around the lanes, or torch beams through the woods; when it rains, splodges of water blur our view, although I think this also reflects the two main characters drift from sobriety. Max stalks them in the dark, but only Lucy sees him and we have our doubting Tom. Max is hit by the car in a jump cut because we can't see clearly. And what effect does this have on the viewer? Bucket loads of anxiety, followed by peaks of fear.

Being simple and short, with a run time of only one hour and twenty-five minutes, is also appealing. *In Fear* contains classic horror tropes, but no special effects or insatiable feelings of grief, prevalent in modern horror, drive the plot. This film harks back to the simplicity of new wave horror where budget limitations led to directors creating grittiness through natural light and constrained camera angles. According to IMDb, the actors weren't told much beyond the premise in order to capture their genuine reactions. All of these choices by director Jeremy Lovering paid off, as the film was critically acclaimed when released at the Sundance Film Festival in November 2013.

The plot ramps up the fear slowly; as things get worse for Tom and Lucy, they begin to doubt each other. Subtle plot points ratchet up tension, but are as restrictive as the camera angles. Lucy is convinced that Tom pissed off the locals when one of them spilled his drink, whereas Tom blurts that Lucy probably annoyed the barman by not giving him what he wanted. Max, the runover victim, adds to their pressure by insisting the locals are after them. Max seems affable at first, but soon he antagonises the pair, culminating in him grabbing Lucy and threatening to stab her unless Tom drives as fast as he can.

The film's structure might be simple, but the ending is noteworthy. The car eventually runs out of petrol, forcing the less-than-sober couple to flee through the woods, where Tom is grabbed, while Lucy forges ahead obliviously. She eventually finds her way back to the car. A full jerry can of petrol awaits her on the passenger seat. There's no sign of Tom, so Lucy fills the car up and drives away. She reaches a new sign for the hotel and it's only five hundred metres away, but it's a derelict mansion in a junkyard of vehicles. Max uses a Land Rover to chase Lucy until he pulls in front of her and disappears. Then comes the shocking revelation: Lucy gets out of the car and checks the boot only to find Tom dead within. A hosepipe from the exhaust has been aggressively taped to his mouth. Tom died from carbon monoxide poisoning as soon as she started the engine.

The characters' lives turn into a jumble of mistrust and fear, then comes Tom's shocking death, and after all that there's still the film's surprising denouement. Lucy has made her escape in the car, navigating the repetitive lanes as daylight breaks and the countryside opens up to her. Except, Max stands in the road, challenging her. She puts her foot down, the engine revs, and the screen cuts to black. Boom! The End. Did Lucy run Max over? We can only guess (but if you ask me, yes, she did). We have come full circle from the toilet cubicle prophecy of the person doing wrong to an innocent being destroyed.

In Fear may be categorised as a psychological thriller by some, but there are too many horror tropes for me to categorise it as such. We have the classic dead animals hanging from a line, signalling ill fortunes. Jump cuts abound, including the often used hitting a stranger on a dark road and then debating whether to go and check on them even though they might be the baddie. There's rain, falling trees, and running around in the dark with no signal being utterly LOST. However, there are surprises too: one being that our lead man is revealed as a wimp, or perhaps just human, another being the derelict mansion amid a sea of broken vehicles. I wonder if the other vehicles belong to Max's earlier victims, or is he just a man who thrives in chaos?

Though in my opinion this little horror flick is underrated, it does have a few issues. The couple driving around the lanes, looking at the same signs, becomes repetitive. And how did Max orchestrate this ruse to trap Tom and Lucy? He had a website and drove the Land Rover that guided the couple to the locked gate, but he was also presumably the one watching Lucy in the opening scene as she added to the graffiti. Why wouldn't Tom have double checked on the hotel by reading recent Tripadvisor reviews? In one way, the film suggests the trap for the couple was premeditated, but in another it hints that Lucy's actions in the toilet or Tom's pint spilling exercise made them targets. Could both be true? Maybe, but it's messy. The graffiti is also frustratingly unclear, but perhaps this is deliberate. Otherwise, the unfolding story would be too obvious. My other bugbear is that Tom would probably pop if he was the only outlet for exhaust fumes, but it's best not to dwell on the mechanics of that. Yuck.

The ending could be likened to the famous (infamous?) *Se7en* (1995) ending, with the discovery of his wife's head in the box goading Mills (Brad Pitt) into killing John Doe (Kevin Spacey) and therefore fulfilling the killer's plan. *In Fear* is similar in that Max goads Lucy into (presumably) running him over after he taped Tom to the exhaust. What's most interesting here is that Lucy is both the victim and the killer; Max is merely a trickster. Why does he do all this? We never know, which I feel robs his character of depth.

Many horror films can scare the fluids out of us, but you forget about their existence once the credits are up. Jump cuts are a classic in-the-moment scare, but unless it's a hot metal in blood like John Carpenter's *The Thing* (1982), you're unlikely to hit the ceiling. *In Fear* shares vibes with many simple found footage horrors all emerging from *The Blair Witch Project* (1999), and many of them play on the idea of being lost in the dark. These films have a purity about them, no frills, just chills. In recent years, the only other film that affected me similarly was *Creep* (2014).

What fascinates me about *In Fear* is how it scares the viewer. Restricted camera angles, darkness and uncomfortable scenes leave us on edge, and jump cuts give us a jolt, but that's not the underlying current of fear that remains when the credits roll. As hinted at earlier, I think the fear this film infects the viewer with is of being lost, literally and figuratively. It is frightening when you don't know where you're going, either in the moment or in life. And what if you get somewhere only to find yourself more lost? There's a possibility of never finding your way as an employee, a partner, a parent or a human. Even the United Kingdom of 2025 is lost after the pandemic and Brexit. We all muddle through as the infrastructure of our lives erodes, because life isn't as easy as it appears in media representations. We can get lost and find ourselves turning into a 'Tom'. He's scared, passive and frustrating to watch, but he embodies what all of us could be. Or perhaps it's even worse if you turn out to be a 'Lucy' (decisive, yet murderous)? If you think Max is relatable, please seek help.

The first time I saw this film a decade ago, it stuck with me. At night, when I closed my eyes, I saw wall-like hedgerows restricting my vision, making me feel claustrophobic. This film remains embodied within the viewer after it's over, greater than the sum of its parts. It's short and simple, but it's also back to basics scary. There are unexpected elements and refreshing gender breakthroughs as well as horror tropes. The next time I'm driving around country lanes as darkness creeps in and swear I've seen that sign before, I'll debate whether I'm a Tom or a Lucy, but without a Max I'll never know. Therein lies the fear.

'Have a drink, mate?'

Alcoholism, Social Anxiety and Loss of Identity in *Wake in Fright*

by Dan Coxon

A building in the Australian Outback, the word 'HOTEL' painted on its corrugated tin roof. Beyond it lies sun-scorched earth.

The camera pans. Emptiness; desert as far as the eye can see. The only feature of note is a single-line train track, running from horizon to horizon. Then a whitewashed building. A different one this time. Neater, somehow; surprisingly so, in the middle of this wasteland.

It cuts away. The railway station fills the screen. Nothing more than a single platform raised on stilts, baking beneath an antipodean sun. The clock on the platform has no hands. The sign says simply one word: TIBOONDA.

* * *

So begins Ted Kotcheff's 1971 film *Wake in Fright*, adapted from Kenneth Cook's 1961 novel. So far, so familiar. At the time, its depiction of rural Australia was considered groundbreaking, but since then we've grown used to seeing the isolation of the Outback, the brutal poverty. *Razorback*, *Wolf Creek*, *The Royal Hotel* – the dangers of Australia's desert heart have become their own trope. *Wake in Fright* predated all of these, but even so, from the opening shot alone it's easily identified as a certain type. Life here is rough, we expect; abusers and predators hide in plain sight.

None of that explains where *Wake in Fright* heads next, or its lasting appeal. Because while there is a hunting scene – arguably one of the most distressing ever to have been committed to film – and there are certainly psychopaths aplenty, this isn't the killer-on-the-loose desert narrative you might expect. *Wake in Fright* is something altogether subtler, firmly rooted in the harsh truths of addiction, social anxiety and class conflict, and it might almost have happened anywhere. It's this familiarity, I think, that has guaranteed its longevity.

We haven't all been stranded in a secluded settlement in the depths of the Outback, losing our money and our belongings as quickly as we're losing our minds – but we might have come close.

I know I have.

* * *

John Grant is a curious protagonist, and Gary Bond is even more intriguing as the director's choice for the role. In the 2017 TV miniseries, Sean Keenan was cast as Grant, and Bond and Keenan share obvious similarities. Both are classically good looking, blond-haired and lean, clean-cut and urbane. Either might have walked off the pages of a fashion magazine; neither looks like he's worked a hard day in his life. There's an aloofness about them too, an innate sense of superiority (at least in the way they play the role) which implies they're not only better looking than you, but smarter too – and they know it. Neither is particularly likeable, and this is the first curious thing about *Wake in Fright*: in its protagonist, it intentionally chooses someone who comes across as supercilious and arrogant.

Do we dislike John Grant, though? No, not at all. He's smarmy and judgemental, overly convinced of his own abilities, but we don't hate him. On the contrary: within a few scenes, we quickly realise that he is us.

The settlement of Tiboonda – and later, once Grant becomes marooned, Bundanyabba, the 'greatest little place on Earth' – is a rough and ready environment. In many ways this was one of Kotcheff's greatest achievements, bringing the working-class farming and mining communities of rural Australia to our screens. It's one of the reasons why the film is still considered a cornerstone of Australian cinema, despite Kotcheff being Canadian – and despite its less than flattering depiction of these violent, misogynistic communities. That it hardly acts as a tourist advertisement was beside the point.

Kotcheff is aware, I think, that these communities are not his target audience. From the children in Grant's school to the inhabitants of the Yabba, these people are decidedly 'other' – strange in their ways, slightly backward, objects of derision and pity. As much as we're repelled by Grant's superciliousness, he is us. Bond's schoolteacher is educated and attractive, cultured and urbane – today we'd probably call him metrosexual. As such, he's closer to the audience *Wake in Fright* played to in cinemas than any other character, and he becomes our eyes and our conscience in this world of brawling and casual alcoholism. We dislike Grant, but only in the way that we often hate ourselves.

It's a delicate balancing act. For his story to work, we need to feel Grant's fear of the unwashed masses, sharing in his social anxiety and his desperate need to prove himself. When introduced by local police chief Jock Crawford (played by Chips Rafferty, that most Australian of character actors) to the game of two-up, Grant's immediate reaction is that it's a simple game, and by implication, easy to win. After all, he's a schoolteacher. His intelligence should trump their classless enthusiasm. For a brief moment, with the beer rushing to his head, he considers himself a god among men.

Naturally, he fails, and fails spectacularly. It's the first time that *Wake in Fright* settles into its main theme: that education and culture is poor currency in the rough-and-tumble world of the Outback. Grant doesn't just lose the game; he loses all his money, cashes the cheque he received for the term's wages, then loses that too. He becomes stranded in this bubble of boozers and yobbos, surrounded by desert, as far from Sydney – both geographically and intellectually – as it's possible to be.

It's little wonder that *Wake in Fright* is often considered a horror film. For educated, middle-class cinemagoers, being plunged into a working-class community must feel like a living nightmare.

*　*　*

In 2007 my wife and I moved to Seattle, in the top north-west corner of mainland USA. The relocation was for my wife's job, not mine, and while her visa was sponsored by her employer, I had to put in my application and play the waiting game. I knew nobody, had no career prospects – I wasn't even allowed to work at first.

I hadn't visited the USA before, and for a while the novelty was enough. The portions were huge, as were the bookshops. I lost myself in both. When we moved out of our short-term apartment and into a rented house, the view from our window looked out across the harbour, towards the improbable majesty of Mount Rainier. If you got lucky, you might spot seals in the harbour, or even, once, a pod of orcas. I was having an adventure, and while there were down sides – I contracted a chronic pain condition which necessitated navigation of America's complex and expensive healthcare system; our friends and family quickly stopped visiting, the prices for the long transatlantic flight making frequent visits impossible – the sense of novelty was enough to balance them out.

For a while, at least.

There's an inevitable honeymoon period when you move anywhere new, but especially when relocating to a different country. Everything is shiny and fresh, each morning promises new discoveries. In the Pacific Northwest, we found that people were almost always smiling and friendly, happy to comment on your accent and invite you for drinks sometime. *It's just great to meet you. We must have you over for dinner.*

Except those dinner invitations rarely came. When they did – or, worse, when we were invited to barbecues and parties – we often found ourselves out on a limb, the newcomers who didn't quite get all the jokes, who were just so damned *British*. I played up to it for a while, using words like *trousers* and *rubbish* in conversation just for the reaction. I was different by nature, so that difference became my schtick. If nothing else, it meant I was served quicker in bars.

There was the drinking, too. I couldn't see it at the time, but looking back it became a coping mechanism, a way of dulling my social anxieties and freeing my tongue. I'd drink to be sociable, and then I'd drink some more. Once, at a party where I hardly knew anyone, and where my Britishness felt more than ever like a barrier distancing me from everybody else, I drank so much that I threw up in our bed.

It's no coincidence that when my *Wake in Fright* moment came, it was through an alcoholic haze.

* * *

While Bond's John Grant is the focus of Kotcheff's film, there's no denying that Donald Pleasance provides its most memorable moments.

As Clarence 'Doc' Tyden he's manic in the way only Pleasance can be, both laidback and unhinged, approachable but dangerous. Grant feels like he's hit rock bottom when Doc lifts him back onto his feet; little does he realise that Tyden's reality is even more brutal and debauched than the working-class pub 'culture' of the Yabba.

It's no coincidence that Doc Tyden is an educated man too. Here is the life raft for Grant to cling to, a vestige of civilisation among the barbarians. Doc is smart, and worldly, and can be charming when he needs to be (as long as he hasn't been on the bottle). In Tyden, Grant sees someone who's like him; someone who can appreciate his anxieties and shortcomings among these crude working men. Both are outsiders in the Yabba. When he's with Doc Tyden, Grant feels a little less lost.

Except, of course, Tyden is a man out of control, an elemental force of lust and addiction. (Might his name have influenced Chuck Palahniuk when he created Tyler Durden in *Fight Club*? I'd be intrigued to know.) Clarence Tyden may once have been a civilised man like Grant, but those days are long past – it's no coincidence that his given name, Clarence, is barely used. He's Grant's Ghost of Christmas Future, a glimpse of where he might wind up if he doesn't escape the Yabba. Educated he may be, but Doc is driven by base desires, unhinged and untethered. The fact that he still treats the sick in the Outback, tossing medication out of his bag like the Child Catcher throwing lollipops, only highlights how far they are from the civilised world.

John Grant, of course, can see none of this. He clings to Tyden as if his life depends on it, and in doing so he gets dragged down with him. When he's with Doc, Grant feels more comfortable, and it's this comfort that allows him to be pulled into situations he would normally do everything in his power to avoid. He attempts an illicit sexual liaison with Janette Hynes in the dust of the desert, only to crawl off her and vomit into the dirt; he drinks and brawls, his white suit becoming increasingly dirtied as his spirit gets corrupted too. When he wakes in fright the following morning, Doc Tyden medicates him the only way he knows how: with beer. As with all addictions, alcohol is both the short-term cure and the long-term problem.

* * *

My moment came not long before we left Seattle. We were already making plans to return to England. Things had become harder, not easier, as time went on, and despite having been there for almost six years, I still hadn't really settled. We had a newborn, and we wanted to be closer to his grandparents. I think I needed to be closer to my parents too.

I was still drinking a lot. At the time I couldn't see it, but looking back it had become a problem. Alcohol became a crutch that I would lean on whenever I was struggling with my emotions, feeling isolated and trapped, detached from the people I met and struggling to find a place for myself. I felt one or all of those things almost every day.

I'd been out for the evening to see a band in the city. I went with a friend, and as we tumbled out of the venue, having had a few beers, we ran into a group of my wife's colleagues at a late-night hotdog stand. They'd also been drinking, and we were all friendlier than we'd normally be. The overfamiliar embrace of drunken male company.

Hey, someone suggested, *why don't we do karaoke? I know a place.*

It made sense at the time. These weren't people I knew particularly well, but I knew them well enough to trust them. They were local, too; clearly this is what people did here after the pubs turned out.

I can't remember if I actually said yes, or if I just allowed myself to be pulled along by the flow. Before I knew it, someone's cousin had turned up to drive us there – with two cars, not one; how many cousins did they have? – and we were headed out of town. I was pressed into the back seat next to someone I barely knew, breathing in beer fumes and day-old body spray. It was maybe 11 p.m., maybe midnight. The initial buzz of excitement was dying down and I was starting to wonder what the hell I was doing.

It's how John Grant must feel, I imagine, when he heads off with Doc Tyden and his mates Dick and Joe into the desert, hollering and boozing, planning on hunting kangaroos. It's the moment that feels most poignant to me in the film. Gary Bond is grinning throughout, but it looks forced, failing to hide the panic in his eyes.

What am I doing here? the look says. *How do I stop the car and get out?*

Eventually, we pull up to a shack outside the city limits. In my memory it feels like something out of a David Lynch film: corrugated roof, neon signs, the darkness enveloping it on all sides. We're not in Seattle anymore.

The bar inside is high-ceilinged and empty, a warehouse for alcoholics. Two old men prop up one end of the bar; a couple of groups of younger men play pool at the tables, looking up when we enter. There are no women to be seen. Someone asks if this is where the karaoke is supposed to be.

No, says the cousin, or the cousin's friend. *That's up the road. I thought we'd stop for a drink first. Don't worry.*

Worry is pretty much all I do. I talk to the two older men for a while, after they hear my accent and decide they'd like to reminisce about the Rolling Stones. Some of the others stand at one of the empty pool tables, though nobody seems to be playing. I've lost sight of the two groups of young men.

It feels like an age, but it's maybe half an hour later when someone asks about the karaoke again. We finish our beers, pile back into the cars. It looks like we're finally heading there. I've lost all sense of time, pulled along by the boozy camaraderie. I'm starting to sober up a little, or at least to plateau. None of this seems like a good idea.

When our car stops, we're outside a Mexican restaurant. It must be the wrong place. The lights are out, there's barely a sound. The cousin urges us forward as he knocks on the door. This is it. They don't advertise it, but it's a karaoke joint after it closes. We'll see.

The old man who answers the door doesn't look pleased. The cousin exchanges words with him, their voices lowered. Some money might change hands. Then he ushers us through the darkened restaurant, the tables set for tomorrow's business, towards a glow at the back of the room. We pass through double doors into a different space, chairs arranged in rows, all of them taken. Everyone turns to stare at us. Half the crowd look like they might be gangsters and their girlfriends, draped in baggy jackets that would all too easily conceal a firearm;

the other half are of an older generation, out of the game but tougher round the edges. They've *seen* things. I'm not sure who I'm more scared of.

The cousin was right, though. There is a karaoke machine, and a panel of whirling disco lights. Beers are bought. A couple of our number push forward to try and sing with a young Hispanic woman. The guy she's with doesn't look happy. I forget which song was playing, but it was probably a power ballad from the eighties; the kind of song a director might ironically soundtrack a fight scene to.

We don't last long. Most of us are uncomfortable, and it certainly isn't what we signed up for. I don't finish my beer.

They drop me off at our rented cottage, pulling away before I go inside. In a final indignity, I can't find my front door key and wind up sleeping on a broken chair in the basement, my coat huddled around me against the cold.

I feel broken in ways that I can barely begin to fathom: cast adrift from my own identity, no longer in control. I want to cry, but the beer has left me numb.

* * *

In *Wake in Fright*, John Grant is never lost. He knows where he is – he never travels more than a train ride away from his teaching post in Tiboonda. If he could pull himself together, we feel, he might leave at any time. But spiritually he is as lost as anyone ever has been: untethered from his identity, cast out among people who don't understand him, seeking refuge in the same toxic behaviours that keep him trapped where he is.

This, at the end of the day, is the terror of Kotcheff's Outback. Not a physical danger, but the loss of identity in a crude all-male culture that wants nothing more than to make you just as lost as them. Until you too accept the Yabba as the greatest little place on Earth.

Always Staring Into Dark Corners

by Gaynor Jones

The girl stumbles up and down a series of stairwells that are suddenly labyrinthine. Strange markings adorn the walls as her footsteps echo. She calls out. She cries. She screams.

* * *

I don't remember when I first heard about *The Blair Witch Project*. I don't remember actively believing that it was genuine found footage, or engaging with any of the now-famous marketing materials. But when I saw it on release in a claustrophobic Welsh cinema in the late 1990s, none of that mattered. It was real.

Like many born in the 1980s I was raised on a diet of lacklustre supervision and video store rentals. Freddy Krueger was not a terrifying monster, but a pop culture figure I cheered on as he chased screeching teens across my screen. I watched my favourite films – *Killer Klowns From Outer Space, The People Under the Stairs, Braindead* – with disturbing regularity, applauding the oozing mess and mayhem. Blood, gore (and even custard in the case of *Braindead*) were easily removed stains on my childhood where the horror I gorged on was brash, bright and bountiful. But as the 80s grew into the 90s, other horrors came to the fore.

My parents divorced when I was very young – uncommon at the time – and I was a strange, troubled child. My imaginary friends were monsters and I still wonder about the odd visions I had on and off throughout my childhood, no doubt spurred on by a combination of emotional distress and inappropriate viewing habits. I developed my own secret rituals to ward against them, such as repeating words over and over, or touching a door three times with my left hand and then my right, compelled to start again if anything interrupted the act. But I didn't grow up in a world that acknowledged mental illness, and the words *depression* and *anxiety* and *obsessive compulsive disorder* didn't enter my lexicon until I was well into my thirties. Looking back now, I remember a childhood threaded with dark thoughts, feeling out of sync. In truth, I always felt lost.

Still, I got on with life, trailing my love of gory horror along with me like a badge of honour, one that helped me push those other thoughts and feelings to the background. But darkness can only stay buried for so long.

When I was young, the idea of being lost held great appeal. The prospect of it as something exciting, floating untethered (and often drunk) through my A-level studies, not knowing what lay ahead. Young adulthood isn't a time for mapping out your life, and yet we are forced to, choosing options and universities. But for me, a series of poor choices led me back to unhappily studying in the same Welsh city where I was born.

In my cramped room I could still escape into horror, thanks to the all-in-one television and video player I'd brought with me. I stayed in halls for two years; commanding, almost gothic structures at the top of the city that have since been demolished. The only way down to civilisation was a choice between a busy main road that added thirty minutes to the journey, or a shortcut via a zigzag path heavily flanked by trees. You can bet which one I – emboldened with youth and alcohol – always chose. Until one night.

It was early evening, though I don't remember the season or the weather now. What I remember most is the atmosphere, veering on comical, the red and white striped buckets overfilled with popcorn that smelled more like sweat than salt or sugar. Seating wasn't assigned back then, and my hallmate and I snatched the last two empty chairs, pressed up at the side of the theatre so the screen was viewed almost side-on. We were hyped, all of us, like we weren't here to watch a film, but to experience an event. We clapped as the screen fizzed into life.

Then, in stark black and white, a little shaky, the text appeared and the cinema silenced.

> "In October of 1994, three student filmmakers disappeared into the woods near Burkittsville, Maryland while shooting a documentary.
>
> A year later their footage was found."

I remember leaning into my friend, clasping my hands around her arm as the movie played out. I remember feeling sick, the jerking camera and close-up shots roiling my insides as much as the building sense of dread. I remember that the whole cinema jumped in unison, the floor vibrating as, late on in the screening, a character ran through the on-screen woods yelling "What was that? What the fuck was that?" I remember craning out of our seats as if we could work out what she couldn't. I remember – more than anything – the sheer terror at the now famous final scene, with the realisation that we weren't going to get any closure.

I have blanked out so much of my difficult university experience, but there are things I remember from that night, post-viewing, with absolute clarity. I remember nearly crying in the taxi home – no way were we taking that shortcut through the trees – trying to explain to the bemused driver what we had just been witness to, why we couldn't walk home that night, maybe never would again. I remember the unspoken agreement that we would not be separating and sleeping in our own dorms. I remember walking to my room on the top floor to grab my duvet and the awareness I had of every creak, every sound, my heartbeat thudding in my chest.

Only one other night from that time of my life sticks.

I am told that my grandfather is dying and I need to get home to say goodbye. I'm somehow locked out of my room with no shoes, no key, delirious with grief. I stumble up and down a series of stairwells that are suddenly labyrinthine. Strange markings adorn the walls as my footsteps echo. I call out. I cry. I scream. I don't get to see him in time. I attend his funeral and return to my studies but wake one night with my body split in two and my eyes flashing. I think I'm having a stroke but don't have the wherewithal to seek help so I wander the halls, alone and crying, until the sun rises. Days later when a friend forces me to the doctor I learn what a migraine is, how it's a normal response to stress, but the damage is done.

I know now that trauma can piggyback, that one terrifying experience can sink, sucker-deep, into another and cause an unwavering attachment. I wonder now, older, wiser, if that's why *The Blair Witch*

Project has always stayed with me. I don't remember when the fear I felt during that movie, or during that awful night following my grandfather's death, left me, or even if it ever did, threaded through the years ahead.

Still, my life did take its expected course – a job, a partner, a child – on the surface at least. But in truth my internal compass is fractured, from a breakdown in 2009, an anxiety disorder in 2012, post-natal depression in 2014, black shadows following me through my life, never quite letting me land, settled, in one place.

But some things anchor me. Horror films, which I watch at breakfast, with lunch, anytime. I surround myself with horror paraphernalia the way others might display photographs or plants. And I find myself rewatching *The Blair Witch Project* at least once a year. Sometimes with reverence, consuming it all at once, sitting in the dark trying to recreate the thrill of that first time. More often, I watch it over a few days in snatched moments, the way I watch most things now that I'm a mother / carer / juggling zero hour jobs.

Back in 1999, at that first screening, I had no such responsibilities and my life was pretty much unmapped. I was eighteen years old and a product of the glossy girl power embodied by the Spice Girls, kick-ass women embodied by *Buffy the Vampire Slayer*, and ladette culture, embodied by just about every TV and radio personality of the time: the holy trinity of watered down feminism. In *The Blair Witch Project*, notably in Heather, I see trace elements of all of these. But there's also so much more.

To me, especially now that I'm older, Heather is undoubtedly the star of the film. I sometimes wonder about the backlash Heather-as-actor received, if the same would have been thrown at a male actor in that significant role (spoiler alert – I doubt it). Of course she makes bad decisions, because – if I can break the fourth wall a little – she needs to, for the plot. But her characterisation, her embodiment of a young woman crumbling from certainty to doubt, deserves more than that.

At the beginning of the film – and the beginning of the hike – Heather is brash and breezy, proclaiming "We are exactly on track". She forges ahead, holding on to the map – and the power. When the men start to question her, she deflects, repeating herself as the movie progresses; "I know where we are going", "I know exactly where we're going", "I know we're not lost". I'm reminded of my younger self, repeating words as if they're mantras, attempts to ward off the lingering shadows of fear and doubt.

But there's a scene later on, around the forty minute mark, when Mikey confesses he's thrown the map into the creek. The stoic confidence no longer holds and Heather shrieks hysterically. I have to confess, she grates on me here, a more stereotyped female reaction, how we expect our horror 'scream queens' to behave. But it's not until the fifty-one minute mark that Heather truly and authentically breaks. The trio realise that they're crossing the same stretch of river, using the same log they've already crossed days before, and the inevitable circularity of it is too much. Heather has mostly held it together until then, on the outside at least, but now she reverts to childlike actions, rocking, repeating, attempting to self-soothe. She is lost in the woods and now she has lost herself too.

Keeping up a pretence while uncertainty breaks you apart inside is perhaps a perfect description of poor mental health, certainly of mine. It fractured again during the national lockdown in 2020, a not uncommon occurrence I suppose. But then later in the same year I acknowledged my bisexuality and a path on the map of my life clicked into place even as another crumbled away behind it. When my daughter received her autism diagnosis in 2023, more paths appeared, more lights flicked on, casting away the dark shadows.

On one viewing of *The Blair Witch Project*, not long after, I wondered if Heather was masking all along – as my daughter sometimes does – convincing everyone around her that all was well until she could peel away the layers and be her true self. But I don't think so. In the confines of the movie, I think she knew. I think Heather knew exactly where they were and where they were going. I think the witch played tricks on her, turning her around, a supernatural magnet disrupting her compass.

Of course, writing about the plot of the film now, on a laptop, with a mobile phone at my side, while my daughter chases digital dragons on her iPad in the next room, the notion of being able to get lost in the first place seems as absurd as the fact of a supernatural forest dweller. But it does happen. Two years ago it happened to me.

I waved my husband and daughter off on their cable car down from The Great Orme and set off to meet them in Llandudno, my simple plan to walk under the cables until we all arrived at the same place. The plan was fine until I hit a gorge, a sudden crack in the hill with no visible path around or down. I felt my breath catch in my throat. I felt rationality desert me. I didn't think of *The Blair Witch Project* in that moment, but the next time I watched it I felt the fear descending, and I felt recognition. Because instead of staying still, or walking to a phone signal, or simply backtracking the way I had come, I took a selfie. Tears spilling from under my sunglasses, my hair windblown across my face. I told myself I was taking it so that I could laugh at it later, warm and reunited and relieved, but maybe not. Maybe I took the photo because it made the situation unreal, made the danger feel distanced. I understood why Heather holds onto the cameras long after the two men berate her for doing so.

I wasn't lost for long, but I've never gone off on my own since. If anything, I think I've gone too far the other way, every move tracked by the litany of messages to my husband's phone – *I'm here safe, I'm walking to the bus stop, I'm getting off now*. I don't want to be like this. I'd love to take parts of the younger me, meandering through that tree-drenched shortcut with a torch, barely flinching. I'd love to go to a forest, to spend the weekend with the friends in my uncanny writer's group, sharing stories and waiting for something supernatural to happen. But here's where my connection with Heather diverges, because the truth is I'm not brave enough. I don't even walk the dog in my local park at night, though that may say more about my horror film consumption than anything else.

But, I take risks in other ways. I get on stage and speak private truths to public audiences, I quit jobs with no firm future plans, I stand up to family members, ex-friends and my daughter's educators in a way which earns me a reputation as someone stern and cold and immovable. I act as Heather does throughout most of the film: brash, confident, ruthless. She isn't amenable, she doesn't bend – even at the very end, she's still filming.

I'm not exactly proud of being viewed this way, but I'm not ashamed either. Because until the last few years, I related much more to poor Mikey at the end of the film – I felt like I was always staring into dark corners. Asking, *what's wrong with me? Why am I like this? How can I be fixed?* I don't know if it's age, or perimenopause, but I honestly care less now. I've turned into the darkness, acknowledging it as if it's a ghost in a horror film – *I see you, now please leave me alone.* I've brought the parts of me I used to hide away out into the light, and I have fully embraced my love of horror, attending events and conventions.

At one of these – For The Love Of Horror – in 2023, I took photos, and people took photos of me. I mingled with people who also love to fill their lives with all things dark, I made friends at the event, and connected with other attendees later online. I looked around at the costumes, the make-up, the sets, I looked at all the people like me.

Also present at the convention were the cast of *The Blair Witch Project,* in the flesh. Of course I've known they were actors for years, but I don't think I'd ever truly let go of that first screening. I didn't pay to meet them up close, but seeing them from afar was enough. I felt the oddest sense of relief wash over me. They weren't lost any more, and I realised, as I lined up for another photo, fake blood on my scalp and a smile on my face, that neither was I.

Get Lost, Spider-Man!

by Daragh Fleming

When you get to know me, one of the first things you'll quickly learn is that I have a fixation with Spider-Man. I always have. And lately, I've been trying to understand why exactly that is.

I can't say for certain when the obsession started. It's always been here really, ever since I can remember. It pre-dates the movies, and later was sustained by them. I'm an adult now, but I still have what many would call quite a boyish obsession. I am absorbed, engrossed, infatuated with Spider-Man. Which is silly, but maybe it's not

I remember, when we lived in Ballinlough in Cork in that rented house on the corner of Sundrive Park for the first four years of my life, I used to climb into one of the trees in the garden and play make-believe with my Spider-Man figurine. It was a simple toy, but I do recall it being an 'official' Spider-Man as opposed to one of the knock-offs. (Note: 'make-believe' is such a gorgeous turn of phrase.) I also had web-shooters that sprayed silly string, a Spider-mobile car that had spiders' legs which moved when it rolled, and several lower tier Spider-Man toys. I had my favourite one, of course, as any child does, and it was this one that was stolen from me, ending a friendship that had lasted my entire life up until that point. (Which, as a four year-old, felt like quite a long time).

I wonder whether Stan Lee and Steve Ditko had any idea, when they created Spider-Man, that he would live in the hearts of so many for generations to come.

Does anyone who creates anything so much larger than life know that this is what they are doing when they're doing it? Probably not. I imagine if you attempt to make something with the intention of it becoming such a thing it loses its ability to do so. It is my belief that things only become so iconic when they are created purely, rather than with an agenda. Once created, art takes on a life of its own, which can neither be controlled nor predicted.

They must have some sense of this character's power, choosing to remake the movies over and over again. Toby Maguire was the first iteration – a perfect Peter Parker, but too dorky to be a believable Spider-Man. Then Andrew Garfield came, and he was the inverse, too handsome and cool to be a believable Parker. And then came Tom

Holland, a perfect blend of both, a believable iteration of both sides of the character.

My next-door neighbour stole my favourite Spider-Man figurine and denied stealing it. Of course, I have no proof for this, but there were behaviour changes to suggest his guilt. We fell out, but my mother, and his mother, said I still had to go to his birthday party the following week. Which was a nightmare. I hardly wanted to celebrate a person who I believed had betrayed me. As it happened, he kicked me out of the party when I bested him at a game of musical chairs. I think he was looking for any excuse to get me removed. I walked home, which took all of 20 seconds, and I could hear the party churn on from my own garden over the wall.

Not long after that we moved away to our new house in the countryside. We never made up, and he never admitted to stealing the Spider-Man.

My mother and father let me replace the figurine with a newer one. This version of the toy had magnets in the hands and feet so that it could stick to metallic walls and objects, simulating Spider-Man's ability to stick to walls. I loved it even more, and it's currently still sitting on a shelf in my childhood bedroom in Cork, some twenty-five years later.

As I grew older, I stopped playing with toys. Instead I consumed comic books, TV shows, movies. These superhero movies spoke to me above all others. While I would happily watch Batman and Iron Man, the Spider-Man films grasped me like nothing else. Even as an adult, I wanted to be him. The movies brought him to life, each subsequent actor giving their performance of a character that will outlive them all. The movies were the anchor, but my fixation expands beyond them.

I've made terrible attempts to draw Spider-Man (I still do, despite my lack of ability). As an adult I've bought Spider-Man costumes, attended new movies on opening night, listened to podcasts, bought figurines to sit on desktops, purchased merchandise, clothing, special editions. Spider-Man has remained in my life, a through-line from childhood to now. I have a Spider-Man tattoo on my leg. It is likely Spider-Man will stay in my life forever. I'll introduce him to my children. We'll watch all the movies together. We'll delve into the animated ones too, which are arguably the best of all the movies. I'll pass on the adoration like a compulsion, the same way families pass on recipes and heirlooms. Spider-Man will be part of mine.

And yet, I've never reflected on why Spider-Man became etched in my heart. What was it about this character, above all others, that stuck with me?

Spider-Man is a hero, undoubtedly. A masked vigilante that strives for justice. He fights crime, stopping wrong-doers and evil-makers. He is special, having been granted superpowers, making him the chosen one in certain respects. He helps people without needing thanks (the maintenance of a secret identity confirms this), which means he acts without ego, or a desire to be famous. Every movie covers this ground. He is, in general, 'good', or at least trying to be.

These are all traits I have desired or tried to embody at some point in my life. To help people without ego. I don't always get this right, but this alludes to the 'trying to be good' referenced above. So, perhaps, I have kept Spider-Man with me because the character embodies a lot of the qualities I wish to have myself.

Spider-Man is also symbolic of unearned power, and what it means to have this privilege. He didn't work to get this power, but rather it was a happening of chance. The spider that bit him could have bitten anyone, and so it could be anyone beneath the mask, which is a core principle that Spider-Man is aware of. It is not about him (ego) but rather, he understands that he got lucky, and so in many ways he is a humble character, who appreciates the unlikeliness of his good fortune.

But not everyone with unearned power acts so graciously. In fact, it is quite uncommon for people with unearned privilege to be uncorrupted. Those of us with these unearned qualities abuse them, use them to our advantage, get ahead by using our advantage. The villains Spider-Man faces throughout the (current) eight live-action films reflect this. The many wrong-doers who are capable of doing good, but choose to do bad with their power. So Spider-Man is the outlier, the one who stands against the corruption, when it would be so easy for him to join them.

The iconic line, 'with great power comes great responsibility' encompasses this idea. Each iteration of Spider-Man on screen handles this differently. While in Toby and Andrew's movies these lines are delivered, as expected, by Uncle Ben as he dies, Tom's version of the wisdom comes from his Aunt May on her deathbed. Either way, the knowledge is passed – the only information a young Peter Parker is given to make his way in a dangerous world with no family. He is lost, undoubtedly in these moments, but he knows one thing – it is not that a privileged life suggests an easier one, but rather that the more privilege and power one has, the more vigilant they have to be, to ensure that it isn't used to selfish ends.

I was only eight when the first Sam Raimi Spider-Man movie was released. Young enough to sponge up whatever ideology was thrown at me, old enough to understand that the philosophy that drives this particular hero is profound. In our world, this idea connected with me, no doubt at a subconscious level at first. That the higher we rise in the ranks of status, wealth, fame, glory, the more disciplined we must be. Because all of it can corrupt. The more power we have, the easier it becomes to allow the ego to enslave, to act only in service to ourselves. And this happens. At various points it has happened to me directly. The ego-drive has its own power, and when we're on top of the game, it can sway us.

Although the obvious attributes of Spider-Man resonate, I think it is this deeper message explored in the movies that captured me. Spider-Man is a reminder to not be controlled by the ego. It isn't a cautionary tale at all times, but there are moments. When Toby's Spider-Man collides with the dark power of Venom, we glimpse how such a pure character can be corrupted, showing us than no one is uncorruptible, no matter how well-intentioned they are. The Spider-Man movies are at times both cautionary and exemplary. The ego can take control, power can corrupt, and in these ways, we can become lost.

In many ways, Spider-Man is an instrument of true Stoicism – to not be affected by external validation, or superficial values, but rather to be led by true virtues: responsibility, integrity, justice.

But I do think there is something deeper going on here.

The mythos of Spider-Man is a classic coming-of-age story. Boy loses parental-figure. Boy gains untold power before an age where he can understand it. Boy tries to reconcile both of these things. The story of Spider-Man is relatable to so many because it is so human. While he isn't lost in the physical sense, Peter Parker is lost without a role model, without a guiding hand. The powers come and he is desperate for a sense of purpose. The reason I think we still find ways to connect with him all these years later is because we all crave that same meaning. Our world has become more and more complicated. It's more challenging to know what to be. And perhaps this is why there is such an ongoing desire to have these movies made, because they speak to us on a deeper level, about something we find hard to articulate.

Young adults are learning that there is no set algorithm. They are realising that adults make this shit up as they go. This is nothing new, but when it is coupled with a world that is increasingly without a moral guide it suddenly feels like a person can do anything. And when you can do anything, it's hard to do something.

I know many Gen Z adults who feel they should never take a job they are not deeply passionate about, for example. The idea that happiness can only be achieved if they find themselves in the exact, ideal conditions may seem a little extreme, and yet it is a common one. Rather than making a choice in the present, many wait for the perfect opportunity to arise, missing the knowledge that opportunity usually arises through action rather than idleness.

This coupled with an expectation for 'specialness' sets us on a course for this feeling of emptiness. Due to the modern ease with which we can gain attention, as well as the previous generation's virtuous attempt to correct the more stern and restrictive parenting techniques of the 20th Century, children born since the 1990's have grown up with the internalised belief that they are destined for great, bigger-than-life lives. They believe this because they see it happen, and because parents across the modern world have told children they are special and unique, nourishing their sense of esteem. It's a well-intended thing with unintended consequences. If you grow up in a home with parents who truly think you are of superstar calibre, it is natural that your world will shatter when you realise that you aren't.

I think the sentiment of this 'specialness' is true, but the execution has been mutated by capitalism and the attention industry. I think we can all have special lives in which we can build rich and supportive relationships, communities and families. In this sense our lives will be special and unique. However, we've taken this to mean that we should all be famous, all be rich, all be living the lifestyles that are shoved down our throats day after day on social media. Anything less than this is linked to failure, to disappointment, and to unhappiness. If our subjective definition of a special life is narrowed to only living the life of a famous influencer, then most of us will never attain this life, and thus, by this definition, will never begin to live at all.

Moving on – I'm not a religious man, but I am becoming more and more aware of the value it had in previous centuries. It gave a tangible structure for how to live in a way that gave your life inherent meaning. Most religious people lead structured lives. They marry, have families, follow the rules, find their meaning through this well-tested life path. Of course, this isn't the only path one can choose to walk, but it worked for most people. And that isn't to say that there aren't other moral structures that can replace religion, we just haven't found one. We haven't replaced religion with anything. So we are unguided. We have no structure beyond our stately laws that inform us about the right way to live. We make it up as we go, and I think without this godly hand to guide us, the feeling of being lost in the world is exacerbated.

We're all lost in this sense, like Peter Parker. There is so much at our fingertips, so much we can do, but we're without our Uncle Ben to guide us. We have no clear paths set out for us. And this lack of direction is what draws us in, because we relate so easily, casually. Because we feel it every day.

Whether Stan and Steve were aware of all of this when they created Spider-Man, if the people at Marvel are conscious of this now as they gear up to make even more Spider-Man movies, I do not know. It's hard to know if any of this is taken into consideration, or whether it's simple math – Spider-Man is popular and therefore a money-maker. Either way, this is what Spider-Man has come to stand for, at least to me. And while, on a surface level, it may appear to be a childhood obsession that was never released, I think it's more than that. It's a symbol to remind myself, and others, of what it means to constantly be in the process of trying to be truly good, and trying to find purpose in a world it is so easy to become lost in.

Ozplotation, HBO, Unfettered Ferocity and *Fortress*

by Adam Groves

It was in 1983 that Home Box Office instituted what, in the words of then CEO Michael Fuchs, "will have the biggest impact on the entertainment industry since the advent of television itself." He was referring to the HBO Premiere Films banner, with which the cable TV giant, already known for comedy specials and sporting events, broadened its reach to encompass feature films.

Those Premiere Films initially took the form of co-productions, with HBO contributing 60 percent of a film's budget in exchange for exclusive TV rights. Features made under the Premiere Films banner included *The Terry Fox Story* (1983) from Canada, *The Blood of Others* (1984) from France, and *Fortress*, an unjustly neglected thriller that emerged from Australia. As with many made-for-HBO features, *Fortress* had two release dates: November 1985, when it premiered on TV in the US, and July 1986, when it made its theatrical bow Down Under.

At least one unsuspecting young viewer – this one – was greatly impacted upon first viewing *Fortress* in 1985. I, however, appear to have been in the minority, as the film has suffered from unwarranted neglect. The scant mentions it's received usually focus on the discreet nudity displayed by its star Rachel Ward (meaning that, no, I probably shouldn't have been viewing the film as a youngster), as well as the rural Australian setting – a mighty compelling sight, as we've seen in countless films, but this one really uses it to great, spooky effect – and the violence quotient, which was unprecedented for a 1980s TV movie.

Critics certainly took note of that latter aspect, with *New York Times* reviewer John J. O'Connor dismissing *Fortress* as a "blood-and-gore exercise" that "doesn't even pretend to offer a cautionary warning about violence." Such criticism, I'm guessing, didn't faze Home Box Office honchos; as HBO historian James Andrew Miller wrote, "The network's programmers insisted that what appeared on the channel be far removed from the tame, timid fare folks were used to seeing on ABC, CBS, and NBC."

The film's mayhem, as with most everything about it, was taken verbatim from a 1980 novel by Gabrielle Lord. *Fortress* was Lord's first published book, written after two "serious" manuscripts were rejected by publishers, leading her to conclude that "if I can't write the definitive Australian novel, I'll try to write a good thriller." That she did, turning out an appropriately sparse and suspenseful narrative with many strikingly gruesome details. The sale of the film rights allowed Lord to devote herself full time to writing, resulting in a string of well received thrillers and the eventual designation of "Australia's queen of crime fiction".

Fortress' primary inspiration was the October 6, 1972, Faraday School kidnapping. Carried out by Edwin John Eastwood and Robert Clyde Boland, who were reportedly inspired by the school bus hijacking that climaxed *Dirty Harry* (1971), the 16-hour incident involved the abduction of a Victoria-based teacher and six of her pupils. Lord's other major inspiration was William Golding's *Lord of The Flies*, invoked by the "*What Violence Lurks Beneath the Innocence of Children?*" tagline that adorns the book's US paperback edition.

My twelve-year-old self wouldn't have known Gabrielle Lord, or *Lord of The Flies*, from Shinola. What did register was the fact that the film began (like the previous year's *Red Dawn*) in an environment I knew quite well: a school, amid children who were around the same age as me. Hence the impact it had on my nascent psyche. Regarding my grown-up self, I find I'm drawn to the adult characters, and the unmistakable echoes of the lone-woman-manhandled-in-rural-Australia trope popular in "Ozploitation" cinema.

Ozploitation refers to the flood of exploitation films that emerged from Australia starting in the early 1970s and peaking a decade later. Paralleling the so-called grindhouse cycle that took hold in North America, Ozploitation tended to emphasize R-rated elements, amply showcasing John J. O'Connor's observation that "These Australians, evidently, are not squeamish sorts." Yet those films also demonstrated a very un-Hollywood willingness to headline strong women, as demonstrated by 1980s Ozploiters like *Alison's Birthday* (1981), *Fair Game* (1986) and *Shame* (1988).

The Ozploitation bonafides of *Fortress* were solidified by its late screenwriter Everett de Roche (1946-2014), one of the movement's major players; among Roche's credits were classics of the form like *Patrick*, *Long Weekend* (both 1978) and *Road Games* (1981). *Fortress'* late director Arch Nicholson (1941-1990) was another Ozploitation mainstay, having directed *Buddies* (1983) and the killer crocodile programmer *Dark Age* (1987) prior to his untimely death at age 49.

Another cogent Ozploitation film is *Wake in Fright* (1971), a seminal entry in the cycle. Like *Fortress*, *Wake in Fright* was a schoolteacher-based, backwoods-set thriller, featuring a twenty-something teacher (Gary Bond) done in by his own naivete and dissatisfaction, which leads to gambling, violence and near-insanity. *Fortress'* heroine Sally Jones, by contrast, seems content with herself and her station in life, even if she, like *Wake in Fright's* protagonist, is forced to work in a rural single-classroom school to obtain her teaching degree (as the Lord novel took pains to explain).

Miss Jones is certainly attractive, being played by the luminous British born starlet Rachel Ward. Her casting came about following a protracted development period, during which the American actress Bess Armstrong and Australia's own Sigrid Thornton were considered; Ward, however, was the only acceptable choice to both HBO and the Australian unions (Ward having obtained Australian citizenship by marrying Aussie actor Bryan Brown in 1983). Previous roles in films like *Sharky's Machine* (1981) and *Against All Odds* (1984), and the Australia-set miniseries *The Thorn Birds* (1983), demonstrated an impressive physicality that served her well in the action-oriented *Fortress* (a good thing, because Ward's attempts at affecting an Australian accent frankly don't amount to much).

The film begins with some tone-setting miscellanea involving one of the protagonists shooting an invasive fox and another nonchalantly walking in front of an oncoming train, portending malevolent forces against which these folks are far from helpless. The proceedings are graced with cinematographer David Connell's unshowy natural lighting, which is maintained through much of the remainder of the film (the effect is broken only by some over-lit night scenes) and accompanied by an ominous slow burn of a score by Danny Beckermann.

Next, we see Sally interacting with her nine pupils in a convincingly detailed classroom setting (kudos to production designer Phil Warner and art director Nicholas McCallum). Established is the unforced authority Sally exerts, with character details sketched cleanly and efficiently, and enacted by some impressive child actors. Among the standouts are Sean Garlick (*Heartbreak High*) as a tough and resourceful young fellow named Sid and Marc Aden Gray (*The Matrix*) as a precocious redhead named Tommy.

The classroom sequence lasts nearly a full five minutes, cut short just as it threatens to grow boring by the appearance of a sawn-off shotgun wielding fellow (perennial Australian baddie Vernon Wells, of *The Road Warrior* and *Commando*) wearing a duck mask. He's one of four armed scumbags, the other three being guys in Father Christmas (Peter Hehir), cat (David Bradshaw) and mouse (Roger Stephen) masks. They quickly round up the children – with the camera pausing to linger on some specimen bottles in the back of the classroom containing unidentified animal corpses (foreshadowing) – and pack them and Sally into a beat-up van whose exhaust quotient is anything but environmentally friendly.

Criminal masterminds these guys aren't. They come perilously close to ending their gambit before it properly begins, by nearly allowing Tommy to escape, having failed to do a headcount during a bathroom stop. Implausibly stupid? Perhaps, but keep in mind that their real-life antecedents weren't exactly Mensa candidates themselves: in the 1972 Faraday School abduction, 20-year-old Mary Gibbs (Sally's inspiration) managed to kick open the back doors of the kidnappers' van after they stupidly left her and the kids in the vehicle alone, and alerted police (unbelievably enough, the head kidnapper Edwin John Eastwood subsequently abducted *another* teacher and her students after escaping from prison in 1976, and botched the job even more spectacularly than he did the first time around, inciting a police shoot-out that left him severely injured and which promptly landed him back in prison).

The poor decision-making continues when the bad guys elect to enclose their captives in an underground cave. There Sally's leadership is put to the test, as are Rachel Ward's acting skills. That Ward maintains viewer interest even when not being chased around attests to a Sigourney Weaver-like projection of strength and femininity, and a welcome avoidance of both the emotional histrionics that characterized eighties movie heroines and the excess stoicism of today's "Strong Female Leads."

Sally's resourcefulness, and that of her pupils, results in the creation of soda can torches, made with salad dressing and shoelaces. These contraptions are used by Sally and Sid to illuminate the cave's tunnels, one of which contains a river (actually a studio tank in which, according to Ward, "We all got colds") that leads to an outside opening. This sequence contains an effectively crafted bit of suspense, in which Sally becomes disoriented while trying to swim through the underground cavern and has to be rescued by the steely-minded Sid. It's here that Ward's "nude" scene, courtesy of a see-through bathing suit, occurs.

Sally and the kids emerge into a hinterland that looks as if it could be adjacent to that of Peter Weir's *Picnic at Hanging Rock* (in fact, the location was the Victoria-based Grampians Mountain range, located 228.8 kms west of Hanging Rock). Not that director Arch Nicholson, known in the Australian film industry as "the fastest gun in town, delighting in his ability to shoot up to one hundred setups a day," had any time for, or interest in, the type of lyricism that characterized Weir's 1975 classic – and furthermore, Sally and co. spend very little time in this wilderness, spotting a homestead to which they quickly make their way. Upon arriving, alas, they discover that Father Christmas and his fellows have already made themselves at home and taken the house's elderly owners hostage.

There follow three killings, of the elders and Duck Mask, who makes the mistake of challenging Father Christmas and ends up staked to an outdoor pole where his head is separated from his body (a scene whose gruesomeness was not lost on my young self). It's around this point that Sally, stationed in a barn adjacent to the house, becomes overcome with emotion and breaks down. To this the action-minded Nicholson devotes exactly forty seconds, invoking an unbreakable commandment governing Ozploitation and eighties action cinema overall: *no mushy stuff*.

Sally and the kids once again escape their captors, courtesy of Sid, who knocks out Mr. Cat Mask with a log. In the melee Cat Mask's gun goes off and wounds Tommy, who's carried by Sally into an extremely brightly lit nightscape.

The group, hobbled by the incapacitated Tommy, ends up taking refuge in a spacious cliffside hollow. There the kidnappers' stupidity reaches critical mass, with Father Christmas announcing on the following morning that he'll return in the evening, thus giving Sally and co. a full day to assess their situation and construct the eponymous fortress.

It's in this portion of the film that the *Lord of The Flies* comparisons come into play. As the scheduled confrontation approaches, our exhausted heroes elect to face down their attackers who, when the altercation finally occurs, prove no match for the unfettered ferocity of Sally and the children. As the novel states, "They had danced around, laughing, crying…take that, man behind the door. Take that, whisperer in the bushes. Take that, bully man. See how it feels. Now you know what it's like. And they had not stopped until the thing on the floor was still."

The concluding scenes return us to the schoolhouse where the film began. Here we see just how Sally and her students have been altered (not necessarily for the better!) by their ordeal, and there is a reprise of the early shot of the specimen jars, which leads to a final freeze frame of disturbing power that I have yet to fully shake off.

Disturbing, yes, but also exhilarating. Arch Nicholson and his collaborators delivered a thought-provoking depiction of childhood innocence defiled, but they also turned out a gripping thrill ride with one of the greatest settings of any lost-in-the-wilderness thriller. Plausibility issues and overdone shock effects aside – in addition to the abovementioned severed head gag we get a leering depiction of a man's body impaled on stakes and, in a version released on VHS in Europe, a last-minute flashback to the climactic killing – *Fortress* rarely ever missteps. It remains an unusually accomplished thriller that in its excitement and excess fits quite snugly into the Ozploitation template, and there's certainly nothing wrong with that.

The Use of the Supernatural in *Long Weekend*

by Marcelle Perks

Films that depict a lost-in-the-wilderness scenario tap into our most primitive fears. We were once hunter gatherers pitted against the brute forces of nature and other predators, and so our fear/flight response is geared towards coping with this situation. When filmmakers use this theme, it automatically ups the fear factor. Most films of this nature typically have a human or monster adversary that takes advantage of the rugged scenery as cover or a trap to terrorise the protagonist. (You never know who you might run into in the backwoods, see *Deliverance* 1972, *Wrong Turn* 2003). In *Long Weekend* (1978) it's the *ordinary* animals/insects/plants and trees that turn against the couple who go to a deserted beach to patch up their marriage. The viewer must throw out all expectations in this eco-horror/mystery/thriller, as you never know from which source the terror will come next. As it says in the trailer, every blade of grass will turn against them.

The most exciting thing about *Long Weekend* for me is that it is relatively unknown, although it was the biggest success of all Australian films when it was first screened at Cannes. This means you might come across it without knowing anything about what's to take place, an ideal situation to experience this classic horror film that makes use of strong visuals. It was shot with an anamorphic lens, using a state-of-the-art Panavision prototype to shoot the final atmospheric scenes as the protagonist attempts to escape a densely forested wood. The way it is shot and use of animal/bird noises on the soundtrack makes for a unique viewing experience. The deserted beach, surrounded by near impenetrable scrubland and trees, makes it the most terrifying place to be lost and elongates the feeling of being trapped in a place you don't want to be. It's not that they are lost in the forest, it's filmed as if the wood does not want them to escape and is forcing them to stay. If you want to see how this story plays out in less artistic hands, just watch the remake directed by Jamie Blanks in 2008.

So, let's imagine you come across this film by chance. You won't know what to expect. The opening is incongruous, the music has a sense of foreboding, the first shot of a crab crawling on a large rockface is odd. It moves slowly, and doesn't provoke fear like well-known scary creatures such as a spider or snake (don't worry, these will come later). It introduces us to the scary place (the deserted beach), although we don't know this yet. Unlike other films that go to an obviously scary location like a cave or catacombs (*The Descent*, 2005, *As Above So Below*, 2014) the viewer must learn from subtle clues where the threat is in this film (later we realise these low point of view shots represents nature's perspective). We cut to Marcia (Briony Behets) who is preparing to vacate her house for the weekend, whilst the news on TV reports flocks of birds attacking and damaging homes. The viewer grasps this is going to be an eco-horror. And it has started… She puts her potted ferns in the bath and waters them (and ants crawl everywhere). The shots of the seemingly innocuous long tendrils of fern foreshadow the final shot of the film.

We are shown long shots of the husband Peter (John Hargreaves), having a friendly chat with a woman; we might wonder if he is having an affair? He is clutching a new purchase, a harpoon which he can't seem to let go of. This fact will become more significant as the film goes on. All the shots of people are frantic, Peter is on the freeway pipping his horn, trying to change lanes. This contrasts with the tranquil slower nature scenes. When he arrives home, Peter runs into his wife's bumper, which he neglects to even mention, showing his essential thoughtlessness. When he sees his wife upstairs, he looks at her through the harpoon's viewer, which he will later do when he sees a van at the beach. It tells you all you need to know about him and foreshadows the tragic ending. Although Marcia has taken care to water her plants, this is the last time the couple will show consideration for anything in the natural world. Marcia, who clearly does not like the family dog, has put three cans of dog food into a bowl outside for Cricket, expecting that to last her for three days. As the couple bicker, Peter secretly smuggles Cricket into the back of his Datsun. Earlier, Marcia has said on the phone to her friend Mark that she is not really talking to Peter. The viewer already knows this is not a promising start to the long weekend and that this pair, who will carry the film in a two-hander, are not likable. It makes us root for nature which seems to be retaliating against them. Although there were other animal/insect

The Use of the Supernatural in Long Weekend

disaster films/books in the seventies, most notably James Herbert's *The Rats* series, the animal involved was signalled as being evil/other, but here we see a thoughtless couple getting the comeuppance they deserve.

Marcia wants to stay in a hotel with friends, but Peter has bought expensive camping equipment. Their idea of a good weekend seems at odds. Marcia appears overly aggressive; although we don't know why yet, there is obviously some issue to work out, which is slowly revealed. The fact that we don't know why they are bickering adds tension as the forces of nature become increasingly inhospitable. They start off in driving rain and the empty dark streets are atmospherically shot. Marcia falls asleep almost immediately (symbolising that when they are together, they are apart) and Peter nearly runs into the back of another van. He also runs over a kangaroo which makes a noise like the sound of a baby crying, which will become a recurrent theme. A lit cigarette end he throws out of the window starts a fire, but he doesn't even notice. These clues showing the uncaring side of his character make him an unsympathetic protagonist.

Peter stops to pick up the all-important beer, but although they are only five miles away from the Munda beach, no one at the bar has heard of it. It's as if it doesn't exist. We are told the area is deserted now the sand mining has moved off. Not a tourist hot spot then. A man who is a dead ringer for Peter looks at Marcia just as they leave. The lights in his eyes turn into the car's headlights on the road. It's eerie and foreshadows the end of the film. The viewer already knows this beach is not the kind you want to visit, especially when they pull up into unforgiving, almost impenetrable scrubland which is on a turn off just before an abattoir. Peter gets out and picks up a fallen sign which reads *Private, Keep Out*. Anyone with any sense would leave. Peter sees the blood and fur from the kangaroo on his car, but if it's a warning, he ignores it.

Despite his wife's resistance, he is determined to get to this beach, even as the car is practically swallowed by the overgrowth and trees which get thicker as they drive – so thick that it seems ridiculous they are even trying. When he stops the car by a tree with an arrow sign, there is the sound of screaming birds. Cricket the dog whines and Marcia finds out he secretly brought her with them. It's another source of tension. And they nearly get struck by lightning. This is anything but a fun trip. Still, he continues to attempt to drive through Blair Witch-type trees in pitch darkness. We know now this is the scary place and director Colin Eggleston makes this extra tense by adding a supernatural feel to the beach/wood. Time is different here; things will decompose more quickly, and plants and the wildlife grow much faster than they should. There's the fact that even though the next day they find out they are about a hundred yards from the beach, they keep coming back to the tree with the arrow, even though there is nowhere to drive to. Lots of things that will happen here are not logical, so there is something innately supernatural, and the beach and its surrounding foliage effectively becomes a character in the film.

The next day, when Marcia wakes up, Peter is cooking bacon on a campfire. For some reason, he is trying to chop down a tree with an axe, even though he doesn't need to. He excitedly shows her the beach, and there's a tender scene where they fall down a sand dune, but when he holds her, she tenses. Something has gone wrong, and surely the bacon must be burning. Marcia realises that it is impossible that they couldn't find the beach from their location last night. She is convinced something is off. There are clues that this location is deadlier than it seems. She sees a dark shape in the water where Peter is swimming and screams at him to come back. She picks up an eagle's egg and spends time holding it, which will become symbolic of the problems in their relationship. There are some Pinteresque conversations with her husband – "What would you have done if I had died. Sold the house, remarried?" Something bad has happened, but they seem to be bad people and we don't really care about them. They litter their rubbish everywhere and there are ants crawling over everything, which she sprays with insecticide. The harpoon (that was on safety) goes off and nearly hits her. A chicken she defrosts is bad. Things are happening that shouldn't be. The fact that the source of friction comes from ordinary objects increases the tension; here anything can be a source of menace.

Peter wanders off on his own. Once he arrives at the beach, his beer slugging, shooting into the air antics make him a character reminiscent of *Wake in Fright* (1971). He throws the beer bottle into the sea, and shoots it (even though they are using that beach and could cut themselves on the broken glass). He shoots into the empty air and then kills a mother duck. We see the headless body surrounded by cheeping chicks. Immediately, he is bitten by angry mosquitos as if in retaliation. Nature is apparently turning against them. Then he spots another van on the far side of the beach. Eerily he looks at it through his scope. Each time he views other human and animal characters, it is in an aggressive predatory way.

When he finds his wife sunbathing in her bikini, he kisses her and it looks like they might make out, but she turns away. We wonder again what the problem is. The beach looks beautiful shot in full sun, but the couple can't enjoy it. We're told it's been a couple of months since anything intimate happened. He asks, "Is it painful or is it a mental block?" They are two abrasive characters who deserve each other and are rarely shown together. They spend most of their time alone, only shouting for the other when they are afraid/attacked. When she tries to masturbate to an erotic book, she is distracted by a recurring theme (the sound of a baby crying). When she ventures to find him, she sees another dark shape in the water as he surfs and is terrified it could be a shark. Animals that normally don't attack do so here. It's all part of the director's illogical supernatural theme. Just as serial killers like Jason in the *Friday the 13th* series have unnatural powers, at the beach and its surroundings everything is different. Ordinary things can be aggressive and behave unnaturally.

Any sympathy we might have felt for Marcia evaporates in the way she handles the eagle's egg. First the eagle attacks Peter (even though they don't attack humans). Marcia throws the egg at a tree, and it smashes, leaving bloody pulp everywhere. When Peter shouts "What's the matter with you, it's a living thing", it's revealed she had an abortion through an affair with a married man (they were wife swapping). She is furious when he criticises her for this – "I didn't need to have an abortion". Now she's revealed her weak spot, she wants to leave and tries to drive off in the Datsun, but Peter has reversed the battery to run the fridge and she doesn't know how to switch it. Angrily, she spends the night in the car and Peter plays a guitar and tries to turn himself on with a Playboy magazine, but is not in the mood. He shines a lamp into the car in an attempt to draw her out, but she only comes when he is bitten by a possum who is eating their grapes. Possums are normally harmless. Now both have decided their holiday is a disaster. They agree to leave in the morning, but it is already too late. Their fate is sealed.

The next day she is up early packing but then goes to the beach and sees a dugong (sea cow) in the water. It is dead and stinks. Peter tells her that is probably the explanation for the crying noises she heard. It likely has a pup somewhere. Like the ducks, this is now another motherless animal.

This doesn't stop him turning on Marcia, challenging her over the abortion without telling him, as they drive to the other end of the beach to see the parked van. The viewer perfectly understands his hypocrisy (seeing as he has made a sea cow pup and ducklings motherless) when he says, "If it wasn't murder why didn't you tell me".

The van is no longer there, and he gets out to take a closer look. Marcia is now so furious with him she removes her wedding ring, which slips down into part of the car, and she realises how to switch the AC. In another startling scene, the roof of the van, that was yesterday on the beach, is just visible in the sea as Marcia inside the car hears about nuclear tests on the radio. Peter goes to investigate the campsite which, judging from the state of the weeds and plants that have overgrown the picnic table, has been there for years. However, there's a vicious dog in a tent that couldn't have been there long. It's another example of the supernatural illogical. Peter tries to rescue the dog, but it's too vicious. Marcia wades into the sea with the gun. Is she planning on killing herself or is she afraid of a shark? Peter grabs her and holds her as she weeps. She waits as he swims out to the van, he sees a dead child drowned in the back. We have no idea where the parents are. Again, this whole incident is illogical. The parents must be somewhere.

They return to the camp where Peter decides to contact the authorities, though just as they are about to leave, they can't find Cricket. Marcia claims the dog died, and she buried him this morning, yet we know this is an outright lie. Marcia is an unlikable character and her hatred of their dog and smashing of the eagle's egg make her seem monstrous. They fight and she kicks him in the groin before driving off in the Datsun, almost mowing him down in her haste. The weekend has been a complete disaster. Peter finds Cricket barking at the beach at the dead sea cow, which has somehow moved to a new position. This is a thing that is dead and rotting, but somehow refuses to adhere to natural laws. Like everything at the beach, it has mysterious powers.

As Marcia attempts to drive through the woods, there are sounds of birds and animals screeching. Illogically it suddenly becomes dark. She keeps driving frantically, hitting unseen creatures. Blood stains her windscreen. A large bird flaps menacingly against the glass. The sound of frantic wildlife and of the car bumping into trees and plants screams at us. Eventually, she becomes stuck in a massive spider's web and abandons the car. We know the woods will never let her escape, not after what she has done. The remaining twenty minutes of the film continues with no dialogue, shot as though a silent film with the scenario and actor's expression alone telling the story. It's extraordinarily terrifying and completely unlike anything you will have ever seen.

Meanwhile, Peter is trying to warm himself at the campfire with his dog. Cricket barks furiously at the sea cow which has once again illogically moved. Peter takes a lit stick and sets alight the sea cow with the petrol from his jerry can. It's a horrible, pointless act. Back at the campfire, Peter is agitated, and nearly jumps out of his skin when a branch falls on him. Nature is taking revenge again. Then his wife's shoe mysteriously falls from a tree, and he throws it into the fire. It's as if he is symbolically burning her too. He keeps shouting into the darkness and shooting blindly. When he runs out of bullets, he uses his harpoon. Things are going badly wrong. Even he can see it now.

The next day we see him visibly dirty and sweaty, staring at something in the distance. There is a close-up of his dead wife's body, more decomposed than she should be, with a harpoon sticking out of her neck. He finds the car, covered in cobwebs, and tries to escape. The car gets stuck in the mud, and he abandons it and Cricket, who is left barking, trapped in the car. He runs, but a snake threatens him. Everything is trying to attack him. This long-extended running sequence is filmed with all the greatness of a Jacques Tourneur scare scene (most of it was filmed using a camera with someone on the back of a motorbike). There are lots of fluid, shaky shots. It's almost a precursor to the found footage films, but brilliantly and atmospherically done. The location becomes the main character and there are endless shots of ever thickening trees.

Finally, Peter gets to the road. There is a truck driver taking cattle to the slaughterhouse; it's his doppelganger who stared at Marcia at the bar they stopped at. Nature has its revenge again as a large bird attacks the driver through his cab, distracting him. Peter is run over. Blood smears across the road. We end with a close-up of the harpoon stuck in Marcia that is already, illogically, completely overgrown by ferns. The scene mirrors the close-up opening shot of the fern in the bath. We have come full circle. Nature has had its revenge. Because the viewer has been encouraged to identify with the natural world and to understand why it had to take its revenge on these two unsympathetic characters, we have a conflicting relationship to the source of the horror. We are chilled by the characters' plight, especially with Peter's extended escape scene, but because the viewer is encouraged to root for mother nature, our feelings of empathy and revulsion are conflicted. Rather than identifying the location as the terrible place, we are shown horrible characters who deserve all they get. This makes for a jarring viewer identification, especially as we are never sure where the next scare will come from.

The standout scene in *Long Weekend* for me is where Peter runs for his life. Much like John Carpenter did with *Halloween (*1978), Colin Eggleston used new technology to make the film more ambitious than it should have been on the $300,000 budget. He used a prototype

Panaglide camera in the last week of shooting to film the climax scene and broke it, but it was worth it. It would have been interesting to see how the rest of the world was faring (with nuclear tests and so on) if one of the characters had escaped. But no escape is possible once you are trapped in this mysterious magical place.

Event Horizon

Why Tearing a Hole in Our Universe is Likely Not the Best Idea

by Benjamin Kurt Unsworth

Event Horizon (1997): Paul W. S. Anderson's sci-fi, reality-bending extravaganza. It's many things, not least an Arthur Machen-cum-Clive Barker twist on a hardcore sci-fi premise worthy of Philip K. Dick or Isaac Asimov. A prime example of the lost-in-the-wilderness genre, it expands the 'wilderness' to not just all of space as opposed to the constraints of Earth, but in fact to multiple dimensions and universes, with all the supernatural ramifications they entail. The end result – for some unearthly reason condemned by contemporary critics – is really quite fantastic. From its phenomenal cast to its special effects, it stands as a nonstop, brilliant gem from the world of 1990s sci-fi and horror.

Sci-fi and horror are two genres that instinctively overlap since both share universes where the unknown presses in on the known. It certainly isn't tricky to find examples of it in the world of prose, nor within cinema: *2001: A Space Odyssey* (1968) relies on it, with its philosophical themes of enlightenment and the Nietzschean idea of something super and something lower connecting in a chaotic middle ground. It's threaded into *The Texas Chain Saw Massacre* (1974) too, with the idea of something innately evil, toe-curling, and so unempathisable being found slap bang in the middle of a world that we're supposed to know so well; everything in this Tobe Hooper feature is to some degree forgotten despite very different, civilised worlds being just a couple of miles away amid the diverse Texan landscapes.

Event Horizon is a film which bridges the gap between the two genres perfectly. In fact, it is invariably a better example of that bridge than films like *Aliens* (1986), *The Terminator* (1984), or *The Mist* (2007), and perhaps even better than films like *The Thing* (1982). After a mysterious and unearthly distress signal echoes back from the Event Horizon, a team aboard the Lewis and Clark – including Dr. Weir, the ship's designer – are sent to investigate what happened and why the ship has re-appeared after seven years. Upon arrival, as is destiny with these things, everything devolves into madness quicker than the Road Runner on cocaine. The abandoned ship's ability to distort space in order to bypass speed-of-light travel has opened it up to a realm of horrors, and the Lewis and Clark's crew soon become victims of the hallucinogenic, supernatural powers slowly unleashing upon our reality. It has to be said that the haunted-house-in-space (as it was imagined) format creates a lot more mystery than a rampaging monster; the pan-dimensional evil lurks in the abstract, manipulating everything and causing both chaos and gruesome ephialtes in all their forms, and so one of its biggest strengths is paranoia connected to that.

Firstly, even the premise exudes the idea of being lost in the wilderness. The eponymous ship emits a signal that sounds like a torture chamber of screams, howls, and various shrieky and blood-curdling noises; it is not a unique factor, with films like *Alien* (1979) also employing a mysterious signal as one of the catalysts, but with *Event Horizon* it is not just what the mysterious signal will lead to – demonic hallucinations, an abandoned spaceship, and various Dantean realms – but the contents of the transmission itself. Trust me, you don't have to be a classicist to appreciate just how terrifying the Latin message embedded within it is (about which, more later).

Sam Neill's performance as Dr. Weir defines him as leading man material, and it can easily stand alongside *Omen III: The Final Conflict* (1981), *Jurassic Park* (1993) or *In the Mouth of Madness* (1994) as one of his weightiest performances. Especially in comparison to the latter, both of which have a collision of worlds where reality and hallucination become interchangeable, it is Neill's intense realism which drives the flow of the story. There is an intelligent, even cerebral, vibe to him, and surely that is quintessential to the lost-in-the-wilderness genre: it relies just as much on showing events as not showing them. Or, more to the point, it relies on showing the paranoia and various mental agonies through which the stories are often viewed. In the case of Neill, this is nailing the more abstract, Lovecraftian elements as well as the subtler moments, irrespective of whether he's playing the possessed villain or the slightly-arrogant boffin.

Philip Eisner's script however employs more than just this as a strategy to establish suspense and an unseen menace; the extraordinarily believable and human characters lend the horrors a greater impact too. Among the sprinkle of comedic moments, every character is subject to a kind of mortal terror. When you consider just how far-reaching the scale of the terror is, the balance of under-the-skin moments and an unknowable expanse created by Anderson's direction are what finesses it. Found footage films have achieved a similar effect – just take the emotional power of *Lake Mungo* (2008) or the mind-bending creepiness of either *The Borderlands* (2013) or *Skinamarink* (2022) – bringing the wild into your living room and introducing the ability to be lost and out-of-your-depth. Crucially, no matter how much we might believe the characters stand a chance or are 'worthy', it forces us to face the thorny notion that there's an ineffable and abstruse horror able to eat us for breakfast, if not something far worse.

As for the guest cast – to play a role as 'straight' isn't exactly ground-breaking. What makes the guest cast impressive here then is the consistent tone they set. For all Neill's intensity, none of them try to upstage him and instead run headlong into their own torments, not least Miller, the captain of the Lewis and Clark, played by Laurence Fishburne. In effect he fills another of the climacteric roles of a survival or lost-in-the-wilderness horror film, since if Dr. Weir is the character through whom we are supposed to feel out of our depth, Miller is the other half of that coin, keeping us from floating around in a zero-gravity of Lovecraftian moments. Fishburne in most roles he plays has that ability to convey everything he needs in a singular stoic expression, but in these contexts one such expression pummels home that you're watching human lives, human experiences, and human motives. Fundamentally, when the more bizarre moments (such as a flaming crew member emerging from a pool of water) hit the screen, you know there's someone to root with. There is a plethora of horror films where curiosity is quite rightly what kills the cat, and we empathise because we understand curiosity – that is what Neill's character shows. With Fishburne, however, while his narrative might be plastered in *Hellraiser* (1987) levels of special effects, through him we see someone who simply wants to keep his crew alive: for instance, Fishburne delivers pitch perfectly after watching a video of the Event Horizon's pseudo-sexual massacre, "we're leaving".

Sean Pertwee, Jason Isaacs, and Richard T. Jones all bring out the flavours of dread that make the survival horror genre burgeon too. While their presence on screen cannot be said to rival that of Sam

Neill or Laurence Fishburne, it would be hard to imagine a film that doesn't capture the punchy sense of rawness without a full complement of actors to each experience their own terror. In the same way that *The Ritual* (2017) is so petrifying in large part because of its four characters slowly awakening to the dangers in the wilderness choking them, this film needs its adrenaline boost of various characters. Although many horror films thrive on an isolated cast of one or two characters, *Event Horizon* takes this to an extreme. In a film like this, where the power of the horror comes from the different angles and a range of senses are attacked, you need the wider cast to convey that the threat is ubiquitous and chameleonic.

Jason Isaac's attempts to chew the scenery, and ultimately his out-of-the-blue knowledge of Latin[1], add something to the dark and depressing nature of the film; whereas the crew demonstrating their abilities would in most films unlock the solution, in this film it only plunges them into a new layer of strangeness. An unspoken descent through Dante Alighieri's seven circles of hell, if you like. Richard T. Jones provides the comedic relief, alleviating a little bit of the audience's tension but none of the crew of the Lewis and Clark's: another display of the futility and isolation to which any horror film in this genre lends itself. He is undoubtedly a cliché, and if there's a loose end among the cast it's him, yet he still serves the wider interests of tension and the omnipresent incomprehensible, eldritch evils.

And as for Sean Pertwee, at a base minimum his character is there to provide one of the best "Oh, shit!" faces in cinema history. But on a deeper level he is probably the most empathisable character; despite every character having something to commend themselves to our pity or hatred, Pertwee seems most removed from the abstract and weird and instead gets a storyline with genuine reactions and deserving of genuine empathy. His character is a perfect demonstration that no matter how much logic you plug into a story of extradimensions and blood fountains straight out of *The Shining* (1980), the madness will always win. And when its demonic punch lands, it will do so without compunction.

Kathleen Quinlan and Joely Richardson, however, join a nice rank of characters that survival horror, be it intentional or not, seems quite good at highlighting. While many blends of horror have empowered female characters in their own way, films within the survival/wilderness genre seem to enhance it to an extra degree. Adding anything from simply female representation in the cast all the way to full-on displays of female superbness, films like *The Descent* (2005) or *The Texas Chain Saw Massacre* best demonstrate the genre's typical train of thought, albeit in two very different ways: the former by including an almost all-female cast to great effect, the latter by demonstrating a 'final girl' who isn't exactly feminist but holds her own against a predominantly male cast. Quinlan and Richardson's performances in *Event Horizon* tap into both. It is Quinlan as medical technician Peters who is one of the first to stand up against the hallucinations with any kind of forcefulness, undergoing visions of her disabled son yet bouncing back; compared to Justin, played by Jack Noseworthy, who upon experiencing such an episode gets possessed by whatever's at work on the ship and undertakes a suicide mission. Although Richardson gets less screentime, she emerges as a relatively human and forceful 'final girl', discovering one of the major revelations about the *Event Horizon* and also being a main player in trying to save Noseworthy's character's life.

Behind the camera, Paul W. S. Anderson is clearly in control of this operatic space-horror. One of cinema's greatest tragedies is both that his original cut was not deemed good enough by the studio and that, worse, the excised footage was sent to the great cinefilm god in the sky. Debauchery, gruesome visions of hell, and body horror the likes of which even David Cronenberg might've stood in awe of – all lost. However, even without this X-rated extravaganza, the eventual by-product produces some terrific special effects, and Anderson does a splendid job of marshalling them into something where the implication is far superior to the splatter.

In fact, the lesser visuals in some ways serve the film best. It's no secret that visuals which leave more to the imagination can frequently be more impactful. *The Blair Witch Project* (1999) is a nice example of this, a film in which you'd be hard pressed to find outright horror elements, yet in a few small moments it hits an atavistic sweet spot, exploiting it to create a terrific spectacle. *Event Horizon* captures much of the same energy. When Anderson can't flood the screen with blood, guts, and oozing make-up, there are more than enough eerily lit sequences to set your teeth on edge instead.

A number of moments spring to mind as svelte examples of this, most distinctly one where the entire tone of the film shifts after a confrontation between Weir and Miller. Both actors give their all here, so they don't need an injection of atmosphere to elevate the moment. But an acutely chilling shot of Sam Neill regressing into the shadows damn well helps, as does his delivery of the line "Where we're going, we won't need eyes to see". Another moment comes not long after Jason Isaac's character has unveiled the true nature of the weird Latin message left behind, during a slice of dialogue from Fishburne: "You ever seen fire in zero gravity? It's beautiful, slides all over everything. Comes up in waves – wave after wave." On its own, that would be a spine-tinglingly powerful image; from Fishburne and with the slow glimpses of the evil they're facing, it is terror incarnate.

Similarly, whilst there is nothing prohibiting the use of SFX in a survival horror film, its sparing use prevents any shoddier effects being at the fore, and allows the ones which are there to best showcase the Chthonic, isolated tone. Thankfully, *Event Horizon* has few such shoddy effects anyway. But the dialogue is still accentuated ten-fold by the effects at hand being the very best and being cherry-picked for the most impact. Scenes such as Dr. Weir's explanation of how the *Event Horizon*'s engine works already have enough energy to be creepy without added input – so to bookend those scenes with glimpses of the vastness of space or the spindly, cathedral-esque appearance of the Event Horizon itself pushes that vibe from creepy to downright chilling. It would be like *The Thing* without those early glimpses of the devastation at the Norwegian base – it doesn't tell you outright the shapeshifting terror which has been unleashed, but it gives you enough hints and brief close-ups of gore to begin your paranoid spiral and realise how in the middle of nowhere and away from safety you are. Or, conversely, it doesn't tell you how the film will end, but it leaves you in this isolated, nebulous void of wondering how slippery the slope towards that eventuality is. In the case of this film, an unkillable sense of dread is there only there because Anderson has a clear-as-crystal vision of where the threat is coming from. More than this, though, he understands how it ripples through the film irrespective of whether he decides to show it on screen.

Another successful element of his direction is how underplayed some of the most crucial moments are. Atmosphere is the true key to unlocking every scare here. During an early point in the film, the Lewis and Clark's crew scan the ship and reveal "trace lifeforms", and they deem these to be impossible and inexplicable. The subtlety of that moment doesn't perhaps capture the jump-scare nature of some lost-in-the-wilderness horror films. It does however capture the suspense such a moment would have, and particularly on rewatch the creepiness of that line infests its way further and further under your skin. It is akin to how, in *The Hills Have Eyes* (1977), suspense is found from knowing something is wrong thanks to John Steadman's character's alleged crazed ramblings, since the question instead becomes where it'll strike from rather than its exact nature. *Event Horizon* subtly establishes a far larger atmospheric force at work first, only some of which is actually shown on screen; both with and without jump-scares, its skill is to make you question not what the exact nature of this force is, but rather whether it will actually strike or whether it is merely the imaginations of the crew going wild. Because Anderson avoids a more finite threat, alien in nature, although it would have served the same narrative purpose, its incursions into our space are far more terrifying because it's all so unknown. Picking an innately-unknowable force from beyond our dimension leaves an antagonist that we can't even *try* to understand, the ramification of which is not a tangible enemy, but rather a war against an entire setting, an entire force of nature.

It's not hard to see that among the many influences from other films at work here, the echoes of the *Alien* films are the strongest. But perhaps the most predominant of them is *Alien³* (1992). In some senses, both *Alien³* and *Event Horizon* are actually trying to tread the same ground. The blending of base-under-siege and survival horror is obvious in David Fincher's film, and Anderson's production carries that across. Both productions use sets in similar ways: almost so avant-garde they belong neither in outer space nor the confines of home. Therefore, when these structures combine with light in a practically symbiotic sense – jagged edges effortlessly shifting into curved ones, etc., – you get an effect that truly alienates you no matter how homely bits might seem. The production designer on *Event Horizon*, Joseph Bennett, achieves this especially well with the set of the Event Horizon itself. Every space onboard the titular ship has a kind of organic energy, and really accentuates the creepier, domestic moments, for instance when medical technician Peters undergoes a vision of her son. Although sets like the gravity drive are full of saw-toothed edges and uneven surfaces, straight lines are actually in quite short supply – everything is curved, or warped, or ridged, or as near to abstract as something tangible can be. By colliding the familiar sci-fi worlds of metal and electricity with the unfamiliar, we feel as out-of-our-depth as the characters in its melee until yet again our trust in what our eyes are seeing diminishes – in essence, the heart of most survival horror films where being unsure of the safety of one's surroundings is key.

Bennett nicely blends styles too to create that sense of unease, not just in the prioritisation of the abstract. When you compare the hypnotic simplicity of the gravity drive corridor, which assuredly owes a debt to the spinning corridor of *2001: A Space Odyssey*, with the steampunk-cum-medieval design of tortuous angles and edges, there is not just something disconcerting and inhumane about each design, but also about the way the styles interact. Certainly, it takes on board the "immune system" analogy used to describe the ship and uses that as its main thrust, in much the same way that *The Borderlands* did to create the impression of a claustrophobic, living environment slowly unmooring you from reality. By contrast, the more functional design of the Lewis and Clark aligns with the down-to-earth, terrestrial hopes of the characters, particularly Fishburne's; it has a myriad of unusual angles and set pieces too, yet it is functional before anything else, not the haunted house of the other ship. Each set is an incredible piece of design; even the minimalist sets such as the *Event Horizon*'s central corridor contain a sense of fluidity, including the brown-green colour scheme, which feels alien despite the supposed technical prowess of the ship.

Finally, the cliff-hanger ending has to be addressed as a subtle, yet integral, punch that the film delivers. Everything up to this point has been treading the quasi-mystical line, and in hands of someone other than Anderson, you could plausibly be watching plain fantasy set in space. Instead, if a final horror-themed punch were needed, it seems Anderson goes back to the *Alien* films for inspiration. Although he doesn't exactly replicate the camera angles and plot threads that the first four *Alien* films all share to a degree, he gives you an unresolved ending which makes you feel as though you aren't actually out of the wilderness. Even the last-minute characters in that final scene go more to disconcert and shock the main characters, and by connection the viewer too. From the labyrinthine contortions of the set to the gothic twinges of the architecture, every aspect clashes something natural and unnatural. And while there are more dissimilarities than similarities between the *Alien* films and *Event Horizon*, through replicating the same sense of shock in the ending sequence, there is a concrete reminder that this is not just science fiction, it is a colossal clash of science fiction and horror, with the horror being the final thought in your mind.

Event Horizon will not be everyone's cup of tea, but do not let its sci-fi shell blind you from its horror innards and entrails. Every shot is composed in a haunted house style, but even more so to put the viewer in a wilderness they do not understand; while it might not go full-on survival horror either, what it knows without a doubt is how to manifest the same feelings of claustrophobia.

---

1 As a classicist, it would be remiss of me not to point out that the Latin does suffer from a slight error – but what can you expect from extradimensional dimensional madness? It should be "liberate vosmet ex inferis".

Navigating Out of the Backwoods

Mapping American Lost-In-The-Wilderness Horror's Evolution and Reconceptualising its Future

by Alex Ringer

Horror is a genre which, since its critically-muddled inception, has continued to pervade American popular culture and its consciousness. It held ten percent of the global market share for movies in 2023[1], and its icons are recognised nationwide. It is a genre that has proved across American cinema's evolution that it will always remain a part of the canon – as long as Americans watch movies, they will want to watch movies that scare them.

Horror is also a genre that has gained greater respect within contemporary film criticism, particularly via the applications of such significant concepts as Gerrig's Narrative Transportation (otherwise known as complete immersion and investment into a narrative[2]) firstly to the shaping and influencing of audience beliefs, and secondly to horror's unique ability, as an evocative, arousing and encapsulating genre[3], to increase transportation and its effects[4]. Horror, particularly American horror, is therefore becoming more widely understood as a potentially enlightening genre, shedding its graphic and tasteless stereotypes mainly associated with the oversaturated slashers of the 1980s and metamorphosing into what Ndalianis insightfully defines as 'New horror'[5], a more thoughtful generic branch characterised by increasing awareness and critique of the cultural structures from which it is produced; especially prevalent within the post-9/11 cinematic landscape (although equally poignant movies, as we shall see, existed beforehand).

On a more introspective scale, horror has been convincingly described by Taylor as a genre 'bringing the viewer into contact with cultural fears'[6], allowing illumination, and head-on confrontation, with the conflicts of societal consciousness pertaining both to the minds of its members and the structures that define it. And as contemporary American society becomes further disillusioned with itself, cinema, and horror cinema in particular, becomes increasingly pertinent to its growingly self-reflective cultural discourse.

It is with this that the lost-in-the-wilderness film approaches the fore, mirroring American society, specifically its younger generation's, ontological state of lostness, especially concerning re-examination of its relationship with nature, demonstrated by numerous thinkers (ranging from Berger[7] to Klein[8]) to be more estranged than ever. And as this estrangement with nature grows, its power and significance is gradually being forgotten. As Badley asserts in his essay on Wild Places, 'natural settings may help us discover ourselves but they also have the power[...] to help us discover something outside ourselves, something much larger than ourselves'[9] perhaps not in some unknown pansophical way, but as a humbling reminder of our position and responsibility within Earth and its complex systems. It is, to rescue the term, natural, therefore, that with their semiotic and introspective qualities, the wilderness and horror have been increasingly married in American cinema as the capitalist war machine has ground forward, physically and semiotically consuming nature and its inhabitants. And via tracking and closer analysis of these uniquely-poised films, their relationship with (to use Lotman's perhaps pretentious concept) the ever-changing cultural 'semiosphere'[10] they were borne out of can be investigated, with these films acting as symptomatic markers to gauge societal views and their evolution.

This essay, in response, seeks to provide a picture of the American lost-in-the-wilderness horror film's progression through analytical examples. Through this, the past, current and future significance of the subgenre may be underlined with its potential to combine horror cinema's ability of providing vicarious, attitude-shifting experience, and nature's tendency to help one find and better situate themself within the world.

'Lost in the Wilderness' is a difficult marker to pin down in American cinema. Its horrific iterations, however, can clearly be traced to the early 1970s, with films exploring influential themes within the subgenre still garnering critical attention today. Probably the most significant, and certainly the most layered, example of this is Tobe Hooper's *The Texas Chain Saw Massacre*[11] (1974; hereby *TCM*), although its first iteration is widely considered to be *Deliverance*[12] (1972)[13], more of a thriller-horror than Hooper's film. Alongside *The Hills Have Eyes*[14] (1977; hereby *Hills*), these movies were essential in the formation of what has come to be defined as 'Backwoods' horror films[15], the most significant horror iteration falling under the umbrella of American 'lost in the wilderness'; existing in deep dialogue with colonisation and frontier mythos, a relatively recent history that still evasively lurks within American consciousness.

Common in these films, as in the entirety of the horror genre, is the idea of the Monstrous Other, pertaining specifically to the backwoods' inhabitants: hillbillies. This is a term bundled with mystified historical prejudice, denoting, as Slotkin famously underlined, 'one who inhabited the physical and conceptual margins of the nation, the abject territory of outlaws, outcasts and paupers'[16]. In other words, the Hillbilly, associated with dirtiness, savagery and lawlessness, is a discursive manifestation of dualistic American mythos and contemporary dissolution surrounding colonisation, and the prejudiced views concerning those who remained on the fringes of the wilderness once it had been "mastered". And as the relationship between modern man and the wilderness becomes more fraught, cinematic portrayal of this icon becomes increasingly obtuse.

In these early iterations of the 'Backwoods' film, the hillbilly villains are presented as a problematically repulsive reflection of urban people, often marked via varying deformities, most famously actor Michael Berryman's real-life Hypohidrotic Ectodermal Dysplasia in *Hills*; in *Deliverance* dirtiness and unkempt teeth. However, these 1970s Hillbillies are also presented with a nuanced sympathy despite their atrocious acts: *Deliverance*'s infamous rape scene has been likened to a vicarious revenge for the earth's rape (including the diegetic damming of the Cahulawassee River), construed by the accompanying pig squealing noises' reminder of human to nonhuman cruelty; the locals, like *Hills*'s "Jupiter" family, getting brutalised by their suburban counterparts in a manner akin to their own crimes. This line between the monstrously-presented hillbillies and civilised outsiders is most interestingly blurred in *TCM*, with the link between the dissociative cruelties of Western society most thought-provokingly drawn.

Striking are the undoubtable similarities between Franklin and the savage Sawyer family he and his friends encounter. Beyond his aesthetic similarity to his killer Leatherface (and perhaps his physical disability reflecting the Hillbilly's cinematic presentation), he too is presented as barbaric in his gleeful depiction of the methods of his father's old slaughterhouse. Acting as a kind of gothic harbinger, he foreshadows Kirk's death when recounting how 'they'd bash [pigs] on the head – two or three times!' and arguably Sally's plight at the hands of 'Grandpa' ('and sometimes it wouldn't kill 'em'), and significantly highlights his friends' dissociation with the reality of capitalism-led animal slaughter ('I like meat – please change the subject!'), a sentiment macabrely echoed by the character known as 'The Cook' (despite his obvious joy at Sally's plight during the infamous dinner scene): 'I can't take no pleasure in killin'. Franklin's discourse with the Hitchhiker underlines these similarities, both revelling in the cruelty instilled within them by societal structures. As Wood convincingly states in his discussion of *TCM*, the lines between 'normal' and 'monstrous' become ever thinner[17], even Franklin's fit after being left downstairs in the old house bearing remarkable similarities to the Hitchhiker's after the group desert him.

The Hitchhiker's behaviour in particular, typified by pathological and random acts of violence, becomes, like his family's crimes, symptomatic of an erratically-displayed, societally-instilled cruelty. His demand for money for his picture of Franklin ('It's a good picture!') is reminiscent of capitalistic striving for material gain, and his impulsive turning of a blade on himself and Franklin depict an uncontrollable desire to hurt.

The Sawyers' previous occupation in Franklin and Sally's father's slaughterhouse is a key facet for analysing their behaviour. Left jobless due to mechanisation (another neverending component of capitalism) rendering them obsolete, they thereby can be classed as what Murphy coins the 'Type 2' cannibal, one who consumes people out of necessity and a refusal to distinguish between human and nonhuman[18]. Alongside his earlier denouncement of 'killin', The Cook's remark: 'Just because a guy has to do it don't mean you have to like it', confirms the Sawyers' falling under this category.

This link between animal slaughter and the Sawyers' cannibalism is a significant one in that it displays the destructive tendencies this societal coding can breed. The manner of the outsiders' slaughter also provides a striking alternative view of animal treatment and slaughter of animals: Kirk's death, as mentioned, mirrors Franklin's graphic depictions of pig slaughter, and Pam's hanging on a meat hook and grotesque preservation further highlights the Sawyers' non-distinction between humans and nonhumans, shockingly illuminating the cruelty towards the livestock they're metaphorically likened to earlier in the film via shots of mud-soaked, exhausted cows accompanying Franklin's slaughterhouse descriptions.

It is important to acknowledge the notion author JM Coetzee posits through his fictional poet Stern: 'If Jews were treated like cattle, it does not follow that cattle are treated like Jews'[19], suggesting when applied to *TCM* that, while the group's treatment is equal to that of the nonhumans killed in slaughterhouses, their suffering – typified in the film's closing scene in the image of Sally, manic and bloodied, escaping the Sawyer ranch – is greater than that of equally-treated livestock. But through Leatherface's lack of distinction in his butchering, the sheer cruelty of these processes remains evident: while the travellers may suffer more on an anthropocentric mental scale than livestock, livestock still suffer this same physical torture; their corporeal suffering occurring on a much wider scale. Ultimately, the Sawyers are a twisted re-representative manifestation of the everyday, entrenched cruelty present throughout capitalist society – an aggressively masculine, unloving family unit; a timely representative stamp destined to culturally stagnate and die, with a grim nostalgia evident in the Hitchhiker's preferences for the 'old ways of killin' and Grandpa, now a withered old husk only stirred by the blood of the victimised young generation symbolising the fading generations that first initiated these traditions, remaining known as 'the best at killin[…] the best there ever was'.

The Sawyers' grotesque home is also exemplar, as Wood states, of 'the border between home and slaughterhouse[…] disappear[ing]'[20], a backwards attempt to follow Capitalist progressions perhaps increasingly relevant today as a criticism of the diffusion of work and home spaces, and of society's hidden barbarism versus its idealistic notions of the home. The Sawyer's home itself also acts as an inverse deconstruction of the idealistic American home, their attempts to reconstruct this with what they have been left concluding in 'grisly pieces of art' made out of human remains, reminiscent of the domestic and commercial use of animal remains, specifically leather, Leatherface's wearing of it as a mask both exemplifying this and perhaps depicting his own form of dissociation from his activities.

Similar to the monsters of gothic tradition, the Sawyer family represent the repressed, specifically the cruelties that pervade much of the Western subconscious. They are the monsters that capitalist codes (specifically unending technological advancement and mechanisation in this case) create, unleashed upon generations that bear the consequences of their predecessors' legacy; displaying backwards versions of behaviours these structures promote, thereby highlighting their inherent cruelty. Their barbarism and twisted exhibiting of familiar notions are a reminder, not only of collective dissociation with capitalism's failings, but also the all-encompassing danger that these instilled cruelties may pose, a danger that Pam's pseudoscientific astrology (despite the disciplines unreliability) importantly outlines as having a kind of transcendent, cosmic inevitability. The Sawyers' scapegoating also evokes notions of widespread dissociative displacement, a tendency of Western culture, to the 'Other', in this case the Hillbilly.

This displacement onto the Other is a trend spanning much of American history that continues in film, particularly exacerbating in the backwoods horror film within the post 9/11 semiotic landscape. The presentation of the cannibal brothers in *Wrong Turn*[21] (2003), a film with initial similarities to *TCM*, exemplifies this. Upholding the characteristics of the 'Type 2' cannibal outlined by Murphy, like the Sawyers, the villains of the *Wrong Turn* series become emblematic of the post-9/11 horror Hillbilly. Their appearances, in particular, are more grotesque, inhuman even, compared to their 1970s counterparts' realistic presentation. They become known only through their disabilities/mutations, as 'three-finger, 'one-eye' and 'saw-tooth', treatment that none of the hillbillies received decades prior. They do not use a discernible language, communicating via grunts and shrieks of joy when hunting the urban outsiders. In fact, *Wrong Turn*'s opening credits, backgrounded by newspaper clippings denoting the brothers' crimes, read like a list of exaggerated hillbilly stereotypes: 'inbreeding; super strength[...] mutation', explained in the 2007 sequel to be due to incest and the brothers' exposure to a nearby paper mill – the latter a missed opportunity to tackle more immediate issues of the Earth's pollution with increasingly toxic industrialisation in the 20th century.

Contrary to its predecessors, *Wrong Turn* represents, in its uncalculated manner, the semiotic evolution (or mutation) of backwoods icons moving into the twenty-first century. Evidently originating from unconscious discursive osmosis with the post 9/11 semiosphere, this dehumanisation and monstering of the hillbilly icon can be identified as symptomatic of an anxiety-filled alienation and demonisation of the Other, particularly the foreign or unknown Other fresh in America's frightened collective consciousness. *Wrong Turn* gains further applicability as an unthinking representer of the cultural climate of twenty-first century backwoods horror when its protagonists are considered: its male lead Chris, a corporate hotshot on his way to a meeting; the young group he encounters travelling to naively (mis)use the wilderness as a vessel for escapist partying, drug-taking and near-compulsive sexual behaviour (evidenced in Evan and Francine's immediate partaking in a sexual act following their companions' departure and Carly and Scott's continuous vulgar references) reflective of the ever-growing use and commodification of sex under Late Capitalism. Its character types are more exaggerated; less realistic and nuanced in a way illuminating the mutating cinematic West under capitalism's influence, both through the filmscape itself and through cinema's function as a conduit for semiotic communication. The result is the urbanite heroes becoming more callous and aesthetically and behaviourally unreal; the same occurring for the Monstrous Other, dealt with in a perfectly-exaggerated Hollywood fashion in being blown up and yet somehow surviving to allow for another money-making spectacle.

The monstering of the backwoods Hillbilly icon can be traced, as scholars such as Harkins[22] and Slotkin[23] have demonstrated, to origins in the confused, often dichotomous ideals surrounding American settlers and the legacy of this relatively recent history. While those who went on to build contemporary America are viewed idealistically as Adam-like pioneers mastering the frontiers (a heroic blueprint often resurfacing in American media), contemporary settlers on the peripheries of the wilderness, through not partaking in the strives towards contemporary American society, are bound with notions of the savagery and backwardness associated with the Hillbilly icon possibly more than ever. In Taylor's words: 'to many[...] the tropes found in hillbilly horror, if not true, may as well be'[24].

This regression is rife in modern backwoods horror, particularly through *Wrong Turn* and its sequels, including its recent 2021 reimagining, with displacement and demonisation symptomatic of the wider tendencies of twenty-first century Western society. These ideals, however, are not represented in problematic ways across the entirety of modern film. In fact, analysis of effective lost-in-the-wilderness film may facilitate much-needed revision of backwoods horror to capitalise on its potential influence. One such effective film (crossing into revisionist-Western and arthouse territory) that demonstrates a demystification of these flawed settlement concepts is Reichardt's *Meek's Cutoff*[25] (2010, hereby "*Meek's*"), loosely-based on the real-life crossing of settlers in 1845 under the guide of Stephen Meek.

Perhaps the most striking image in *Meek's* is that which is most broadly applicable to the lost-in-the-wilderness film as a whole: the word 'Lost' itself, carved into a tree-trunk by Paul Dano's Thomas Gately; as Gorfinkel states: 'a proclamation of a diegetic place, a location in narrative time, and perhaps an existential state'[26], a state, as discussed, ever-more applicable to current Western society. It is also a diegetically permanent state, with the characters making no definitive progress in their major goal of searching for water from the opening of the film to its close. They're presented as diminutive; helpless to the indifferent will of the wilderness, and are shot to look miniscule against incredibly vast, barren landscapes, no nourishment or familiar civilisation present anywhere.

Meek's striking anachronism contributes largely to its demystification of frontier narratives, its long, meditative shots of arduous walking, working and general lack of progress blurring any sense of time and advancement; chipping slowly away at the mythologies surrounding settlement alongside its alternate, uncompromising female perspective, with the audience, like the female settlers, obscured from their ultimately incompetent male leaders' discussions. And it is the mythology surrounding the masculine Western settler/hero that is most effectively deconstructed in the film via this unique perspective, alongside its presentation of the character of Stephen Meek. A revisionist play on the heroes of classic Westerns, Meek is presented as a fraud who is gradually exposed for his lack of knowledge; of the inherent mastery of his vast surroundings that early characters of his archetype inexplicably exhibit in Western films. As the group loses faith in him, his outrageous tales (such as of his friend's killing of a bear within the lands, itself suggestive of celebrated barbarism associated with toxic masculinity) impress the group less and less. And Meek's racially-charged murderousness towards the native the group finds, reminiscent of the cowboy-versus-Indian trope in Western media, is overruled as he is ousted by Emily Tetherow, who recognises the superior knowledge of the native over the naive settler.

Importantly, the film avoids idealism in the oppressed Emily Tetherow's takeover, authentically presenting her belief of cultural superiority to the native they encounter. At first, she in some way buys into Meek's assertion that the American natives are 'nothing more than animals[...] savages' (an example of early demonisation of the Other in American history), attempting to shoot him on first sighting. And once he is captured, the aid she gives him is purely transactional: 'I want him to owe me something' despite his only plight coming at her group's hands, the forced creation of a debt so prevalent in the history of natives and oppressive settlers, even Emily herself exhibiting, quite ironically in the moment, their belief of superiority: 'You cannot imagine the things we've done... the cities we've built', insistent on communicating to him in an alien language despite the group's increasing reliance on him and their equal presence within the dwarfing, barren landscape. The group are left at the mercy of the native and his sense of direction, with it unclear if he even understands what he is leading them to, and this is unconcluded in an enigmatic presentation of the wilderness as a dwarfing, overcoming plain (and, in the sense of a level of existence, plane) which the characters can barely navigate. With this Reichardt achieves a demystification of the masculine frontier hero, as well as wider frontier mythology denoting Western superiority and visionary mastery of the wilderness versus native savagery.

The importance and applicability of *Meek's Cutoff*'s backwoods revision is biramous, firstly in its demystification of the typical Western hero as a key facet of frontier mythos and reversal of this icon into a villainous role, and secondly in its accompanying unique perspective and its uncompromising nature, imperative to approaching such layered concepts through a new lens. It can therefore be suggested to apply to future depictions of the backwoods which are routed in this biased mythology, with similarly effective demystification of prejudiced beliefs perhaps being achievable via reversal of the Hillbilly as villain and outsider as hero, and the provision of an alternative perspective of the settled rather than the intruder.

Demystification is also a theme which bleeds into other forms of the lost-in-the-wilderness horror film, particularly within the found-footage sector. Popularised by *The Blair Witch Project*[27] (1999), found-footage horror typically explores beliefs in cryptids, a mythology particularly tied to rural America. Demystification, or re-mystification (a process increasingly explored in contemporary ecocriticism) is often presented as a kind of battlefield for the characters in these films. Often low-budget, they typically feature a similar narrative trend to other lost-in-the-wilderness horror – that is, naive characters straying too far into the wilderness and meeting something that is far beyond them.

As in *Blair Witch*, this straying into the wilderness is often in search of a mythological being (in this case, the Blair Witch itself), and in other such films a cryptid, such as in *Willow Creek*[28] (2013), with financial gain and/or gain of fame a consideration, alongside vaguer notions of discovering the truth about the myths. *Willow Creek* is charged with an unnerving sense of voyeurism, as well as exploitation, on the part of the characters themselves in their intention to use nature and its potential inhabitants for their own gain, but also on the part of the viewer, given an unusual, non-consensual view into characters' plight.

The monsters that are encountered (albeit in inconclusive ways) can be viewed, similarly to the hillbillies of the backwoods, or general horror monsters, as manifestations; representations of the repressed. Cryptids, and the creatures of the wilderness, specifically act as a manifestation of nature's anger at its trespassers, allowing it to fight back. The characters of these films are therefore punished for their intended exploitation of nature, and their naive beliefs of mastery over it, similarly to films like *Meek's Cutoff*, but with a horrific twist. The viewer's role isn't forgotten either, with most of these films imbued with a raw, unfiltered feel through mis-takes and audio faults purposefully included (such as in *Willow Creek's* opening scene), reminding us of our own everyday intrusiveness.

This notion is interestingly evident in *Willow Creek*'s longest scene, a thirteen-minute take of couple Jim and Kelly being terrorised by an unseen sasquatch. In search of the location of the famed Patterson-Gimlin footage ("Bigfoot" itself also being a quintessential emblem of US monster-culture and the fanaticism surrounding it) the couple, who experience personal trouble between them during the trip (another common trope in these films highlighting nature's ability to bring these meditative issues to the fore), become lost and are forced to set up camp in this unknown and treacherous location. And in this scene, tactfully authentic in a manner similar to *Meek's* meditative style, tension is rife due to the limited view of the characters' reactions to the sasquatch outside and what it does to the tent, it becomes clear that no longer is the hunt for "Bigfoot" being presented here, but instead the hunt of humans by it. This role-reversal garners a further irony in the movie's close, where a brief shot of a humanoid creature is followed by the off-screen deaths of Jim and Kelly. On their trip that Jim was so insistent on, the couple have paid with their lives for what ultimately is a dubious mix of that split-second shot and the cries of distant sasquatches. *Willow Creek* and films like it borrow *Blair Witch*'s aesthetics to show that not only may the wilderness hold within it things that we have not yet seen, but, in a trend increasingly prevalent in nature documentaries such as *Silent Roar* [29], it also demonstrates that perhaps this should remain that way. Unlike modern backwoods films such as *Wrong Turn*, a (perhaps unfortunate) comeuppance for naive behaviour rooted in arrogant mythos from the wilderness itself rather than presented as unaware victims being gruesomely picked off by a monstrous, foreign Other, acting as a warning that the wilderness and its inhabitants are not below humanity and must be respected.

The wilderness and its inhabitants are complicated notions within the American canon, but are nevertheless evidently explorable and unpickable through film. It is possible that through mapping and analysis of the evolution of their presentation in horror and other genres that the problematic regression of this presentation may be revised and rethought, allowing for alternative and nuanced perspectives to be portrayed and the influential power of lost-in-the-wilderness horror to be fully realised. Through vicariously experiencing and considering lostness, our dissolution with contemporary societal structures and tendencies, our relationship to nature and its inhabitants, and our repressed cruelties, can be recognised and examined. Through providing narratives with enlightening perspectives, demystification, and revision of stereotyped icons, lost-in-the-wilderness horror may provide an important navigator through the wilderness of American cultural consciousness.

Endnotes

1 According to 'thenumbers.com' https://www.the-numbers.com/market/genre/Horror Accessed 09/07/2024

2 Defined by Green, MC. (2008), in 'Transportation Theory' in *The International Encyclopedia of Communication*, Donsbach, W. (ed.) https://doi.org/10.1002/9781405186407.wbiect058

3 See: Ballenghein, et al. (2023); Jacobs et al. (2015); Hsu, et al. (2014)

4 See: Green, MC. (2021); Green, MC; Brock, TC; Kaufman, G. (2008); Green, MC. (2008)

5 In: Ndalianis, A. 'Gender, Culture and the Semiosphere: New Horror Cinema and Post 9/11' in *International Journal of Culture Studies*, 18:1 (2015)

6 Taylor, T. 'Hillbilly Horror' in *The Palgrave Handbook of Contemporary Gothic*, ed. Bloom, C. (Palgrave Macmillan: London, 2020)

7 See: Berger, J. 'Why Look at Animals?' (Penguin: London, 2009)

8 See: Klein, N. 'This Changes Everything: Capitalism vs the Climate' (Penguin: London, 2015)

9 Badley, K. 'Nature, Wilderness and Discovery of the Self- The Spirituality of Wild Places' in *Education: An Interdisciplinary Approach to Nature*, ed. Etherington, K (Wipf and Stock: Eugene, Oregon, 2023), p.113

10 See: Lotman, J; Clark, W. 'On the semiosphere' in *Signs Systems Studies* (2005), 33:1, 205-229

11 Hooper, T. 'The Texas Chain Saw Massacre' (Louis Peraino of Bryanston, 1974)

12 Boorman, J. 'Deliverance' (Warner Bros. Pictures, 1972)

13 See: Hervey, B. 'Contemporary Horror Cinema' in *The Routledge Companion to Gothic*, eds. Spooner, C; McEvoy E (Routledge:Oxfordshire, 2007); Wood, R. 'Hollywood from Vietnam to Regan... and beyond' (Columbia University Press: New York City, New York, 2003)

14 Craven, W. 'The Hills Have Eyes' (Vanguard, 1977)

15 Particularly by Murphy, BM. in 'The Rural Gothic in American Popular Culture: Backwoods Horror and Terror in the Wilderness'

16 Slotkin, R. 'Regeneration through Violence: The Mythology of the American Frontier', New edition (University of Oklahoma Press: Norman, Oklahoma, 2000) p.134-135

17 Wood, R. p.83

18 Murphy, BM. p.149-150

19 Coetzee, JM. 'The Lives of Animals' (Princeton University Press: Princeton, New Jersey, 1999) p.49-50

20 Wood, R. p.83

21 Schmidt, R. 'Wrong Turn' (Twentieth Century Fox, 2003)

22 Harkins, A. 'Hillbilly: A Cultural History of an American Icon' (Oxford University Press USA: New York City, New York, 2005)

23 Slotkin, R. 'Regeneration through Violence: The Mythology of the American Frontier'

24 Taylor, T. p.176

25 Reichardt, K. 'Meek's Cutoff' (Oscilloscope Pictures, 2010)

26 Gorfinkel, E. 'Exhausted Drift: Austerity, Dispossession and the Politics of Slow in Kelly Reichardt's *Meek's Cutoff* in *Slow Cinema* (2016), eds. De Luca, T; Barrabas Jorge, N. p.128

27 Sanchez, E; Myrick, D. 'The Blair Witch Project' (Artisan Entertainment, 1999)

28 Goldthwaite, B. 'Willow Creek' (Dark Sky Films, 2013)

29 Kelly, M; Miles, H. 'Silent Roar' (USA Public Broadcasting Service, 2005)

Ravenous

Deus Absconditus

by Lisa Moore-Smith

I

Lost is a complicated notion. In the fairy tales we read as children, if nobody gets lost, the story never starts. For the Orphan, the Prince, or the Handless Maiden, *lost* is the path to finding their real selves. When we're young we intuit this, and don't really fear for them. The Handless

Maiden will find the clockmaker who builds her better hands, the brambles will open before the Prince so he can rouse his anima with a kiss, and the Orphan finds its true parentage.

In the horror genre, of course, *lost* is something darker.

The world of Shirley Jackson so entirely unsettles because her characters keep finding themselves coming unstuck into lostness, even amid the familiar: in one's own city, one's own backyard. Smiling faces, family-members and lovers turn without warning into utter strangers. The mask falls, and behind it is menace. It's sudden, and yet *it has been there all along*. In *Hangsaman*, a girl sits in her dorm-room at night. She wants to keep the lights off because it makes things "beautiful and shadowy", but she's worried what people will think, so on go the lights, and suddenly it's all sharp corners, and "the feet of the desk on the floor were somehow obscene". Malevolence is always present. It's normally hidden, until it's not. That is the treachery of the familiar.

Then there's the other kind of landscape, the one that is entirely alien, dangerous in its passivity, blind and uncaring. The side of Nature which she waits to show us until we are lost, and at her mercy.

* * *

II: EXCELLENT SCENES, PART ONE

You're lying broken at the bottom of the world. The strongest man you've ever known is dead beside you. A madman is on the prowl, looking to eat you. A major bone protrudes from your leg. Through the web of fallen tree-limbs, you can see the moon, and it is gorgeous.

Ravenous director Antonia Bird lets us watch it. For one long, dazzling moment, it's like we're in a Terence Malick movie.

But here's the thing: as lovely as the moon is, it's not going to interfere when someone wants to eat you.

* * *

III

I like it when genres entangle. I like it when a pirate movie has seamonsters, or cowboys fight aliens, or zombies clear out a Nazi bunker.

Ravenous is one of these. It's the most exhilarating cannibal gorefest you'll ever see, and it's all dressed up like a western/war picture. It's *Dances with Wolves*, except the monsters of the indigenous myths are real and embodied in the infected, rapacious, white-man gluttons who wear blue uniforms and consume entire peoples. They want to eat the whole landscape, and anyone who strays across their mad path.

All the best horror films succeed on two levels: not only a superior story superbly told, but one with a working allegory, as well. Would we still remember *Night of the Living Dead* if the hero was played by a white guy? Maybe – such are the talents of George Romero – but it wouldn't haunt us as it does.

Ravenous is a master-course in playing these two levels as a dance, back and forth, with humor and historical irony and endless, endless buckets of blood, all the way to its astonishingly powerful climax. ("We ran out of prop blood," Bird says in her DVD commentary. "We were using gallons of it every day. It just kind of slides into the earth.")

The allegory in this case is Manifest Destiny. The monster in this monster-movie is called by the Natives *wendigo*, a sort of Hungry Ghost with an insatiable appetite. One man swallows the flesh of another, captures his strength, feels it surge within him, and becomes addicted. Once he's tasted of this Fatal Goor, his blood-lust will not be controlled.

* * *

"Jacob Donner's wife came down the steps one day saying to mother 'What do you think I cooked this morning?' then answered the question herself, 'Shoemaker's arm.'"
—excerpt from a letter by Donner Party survivor Mrs. W.A. Babcock, 15 June 1879.

* * *

IV: EXCELLENT SCENES, PART TWO

Three army officers sit in a cozy parlor around a kettle of man-flesh stew. Two are cannibals and the third is dying, his blood gurgling from both mouth and slit gut.

With twinkling eye, one cannibal says: "Well. Isn't this civilized?"

* * *

"...in the act of devouring him they accomplished their identification with him, and each one of them acquired a portion of his strength."
—Sigmund Freud, *Totem and Taboo*

* * *

V

We begin with a flawed man, a coward dressed as a hero.

He is Boyd, played by Guy Pearce, and it's a time of war: the U.S. versus Mexico. Boyd is a lieutenant, and spectacularly ill-suited to his job. In the midst of the uber-violent massacre in which his entire unit winds up dead, he lies down and plays possum, letting himself be dragged into the stack of corpses. Wedged between his dead comrades, he accidentally swallows the blood and brains of his ex-commanding officer, and *something happens*. It makes him strong, makes him super-animal. For a little while, it makes him Other. This is the fulcrum upon which our story turns. He crawls from his grotesque charnel-stack and takes the enemy fortress single-handed.

All this we see in flashback. By the time we meet him, he is once again sheepish, diffident, and miserably conscious of his own craven nature. At the supper in his honor, he cannot look at the bloody steak on his plate without retching. He has gained a promotion and a medal, bestowed cynically by his general because it would "set a bad precedent" to punish him outright. Instead, our flawed man's punishment is to be posted to the very edge of the world: to a tiny, isolated fortress amidst the snows of the California Sierras.

Donner Party country.

The bulk of this movie was shot in Slovakia, and the isolation feels genuinely unbreachable. You well believe that here is nothing but ice and caverns of yawning death and no mercy at all, all the way to the horizon and beyond.

The personnel mustered in this frozen, claustrophobic outpost are few and singular, each a misfit in his own way. Colonel Hart (Jeffrey Jones) reads philosophy in dead languages.

Major Knox (Stephen Spinella) has his bottle, Private Tofler (Jeremy Davies) his hymn-making and prayers. Private Cleaves (David Arquette) is a simpleton who needs only his weed to make him happy, and Private Reich (Neal McDonough) is the perfect soldier, all sinew and discipline, with not an ounce of doubt or sentiment.

The hired hands are indigenous siblings, Martha (Sheila Tousey) and George (Joseph Running-Fox). Naturally, they watch the events unfold from a different perspective. Sometimes you can't see your own madness until it's reflected in an objective eye, as Boyd understands when he approaches Martha for help. In her revulsion he sees clearly his own monstrosity, and she has no hope to offer him. There's nothing to be done. A leopard and its spots are stuck together until death do them part.

But the real trouble starts when a half-naked Scotsman (Robert Carlyle) staggers into camp one stormy night, telling an awful tale of a lost wagon-train and anthropophagy.

* * *

"Frid 26th froze hard last night   today clear & warm Wind S:E: blowing briskly. Marthas jaw swelled with the toothache: hungry times in camp, plenty hides but the folks will not eat them we eat them with a tolerable good apetite. Thanks be to Almighty God. AMEN Mrs Murphy said here yesterday that (she) thought she would Commence on Milt. & eat him. I don't (think) that she has done so yet, it is distressing The Donnos told the California folks that they (would) commence to eat the dead people 4 days ago… I suppose they have done so ere this time.

Satd 27th beautiful morning sun shining brilliantly, wind about S.W."
 —diary of Donner Party member Patrick Breen, 1846

* * *

VI

Every element of *Ravenous* is stellar, from casting to production design. The script is an unpretentious gem, and Nyman and Albarn ought to have won an Oscar for the music. During the initial pursuit of the cannibal, in which it's comically unclear who's chasing whom, the music sounds like an Appalachian turkey-hunt. Even better, there is a recurring martial theme played on the least bellicose instruments conceivable: it sounds like it's thumped out on a wash-tub, a toy piano, a wheezy accordion, and a one-string gourd by a couple of guys on a porch-swing. It's brilliant. It's the perfect undercurrent for a movie that makes you laugh and scares you crapless, simultaneously.

That's a tough trick to carry off even once or twice, but here, Bird manages it several times. After you've seen it, I *dare* you to try and forget Robert Carlyle's manic fit in the snow outside the cave, or Jeremy Davies' anguished cry, "He was licking me!" Or the marvelous endgame, in which two men caught in a bear-trap are playing Whoever-Dies-First-Gets-Eaten.

The bulk of the humor comes from Robert Carlyle, with his irrepressible, bloody-mouthed, flesh-rending playfulness. It's both grotesque and familiar, because at some point you realize this is how your own sweet house-moggy would be, if it could talk and preferred eating the flesh of other cats. Carlyle is the very picture of the amoral blood-luster having a little pre-prandial game with his food.

* * *

VII: EXCELLENT SCENES, PART THREE

When Boyd first arrives at the fort, he meets with Colonel Hart, a genial, bookish man.

"Funny thing," the colonel says. "Escape the world. Come here. Turn right around and try to escape this place. The thing about escape, though, you might end up someplace worse."

Later, the same man will say, "It's lonely being a cannibal. Tough to find friends."

* * *

"No man is a philanthropist on the prairie."
—Francis Parkman, *the Oregon Trail*

* * *

VIII

If you google "taking in the soul by eating the flesh", what you get is a long list of exegesis on John 6:53 ("I tell you the truth, unless you eat the flesh of the Son of Man and drink his blood, you have no life in you"). In 6:54, John follows it up with what you might call this movie's satirical and slightly blasphemous slogan: "Whoever eats my flesh and drinks my blood has eternal life."

The Cannibal, most often in its undead Zombie form, has dethroned the Vampire to become this century's pet metaphor in horror cinema. Vampirism will return, of course, it always does, but the ground has been over-harvested and must lie fallow awhile. In the meantime, the ilk of Sawney Beane and Sweeney Todd wreak their havoc while teaching us lessons about the dismal swamplands within our own souls. The Cannibal's allegorical bailiwick overlaps much of the territory to which vampirism has laid traditional claim: addiction, debauchery, class oppression, and emotional dysfunction via *poisoned blood*, or familial legacy. The recent film *Bones and All* (2022; dir. Luca Guadagnino), featuring a wildly disturbing performance by Mark Rylance, plays in the muck of this latter, giving us a sub-race of humans who are genetically disposed to eat the ones they love. The Catholic intellectual-mystic Simone Weil once defined friendship as "a miracle by which a person consents to view from a certain distance, and without coming any nearer, the very being who is as necessary to him as food." These words could be the central complaint of Rylance's kin, the "Eaters", as they call themselves.

If you let them close enough, sooner or later, it's supper-time.

* * *

IX: EXCELLENT SCENES, PART FOUR

"Morality," the new colonel sneers at Boyd. "The last bastion of a coward."

Then he drives a dagger into his guts.

* * *

X

The sanguinary Colonel Ives takes a moment to reflect aloud on Manifest Destiny, and the gold-seekers who are coming – to dinner, if the colonel has his way. "This country is seeking to be whole," he says. "Stretching out its arms and consuming all it can. And we merely follow."

This landscape is a presence. The mountains beyond the tiny fort are jagged, violent-looking, inconceivably tall. From every angle this place is bleak, cold and forbidding, even terrifying in its desolate majesty. You don't want to look at it too long. It is a character in itself, one that leaves its mark on every scene.

It even feels *conscious*, this land, although it would be a mistake to call it malevolent. Rather, its presence is an amoral one, awesome yet removed, passively consensual, much like the *Deus Absconditus* of Mel Gibson's *The Passion of the Christ*, a God withdrawn from a world through which Satan parades in open triumph.

* * *

XI

I end with a personal confession:

I first saw this movie when it was released on DVD, because it was received so poorly at the local cinema it was gone before I knew it was there.

At this time, I'd been a vegetarian for some years.

After the final shots, after the General eats from the kettle and the woman stumbles, horrified, away into the wasteland of ice which suddenly seems safer than this blood-painted abattoir of dead horses and pale-faced monsters, as I listened to that buoyant, meandering, pseudo-martial tune, and as the camera rose slowly up and away from the corpses left in the wake of Boyd's Pyrrhic victory, I was left feeling a little drunk.

I stepped outside and looked up at the waxing moon. My senses were sharpened. It was summer-time, and I could smell some night-blooming flower I'd never noticed before. I felt a strange giddiness and thought, "I want to eat raw meat. I wish I was a werewolf."

That's all. There's no postscript. I went to bed and slept it off, and was still vegetarian when I woke. My point is this: some movies leave you feeling like you're on an acid trip.

Ravenous is one of those.

* * *

"never take no cutofs and hury along as fast as you can."
--letter from Donner Party survivor Virginia Reed, 16 May 1847

All Sinners Are Lost

The Art of Being Lost in *As Above, So Below*

by Sarah R New

© Legendary Entertainment

In the survival horror sub-genre, getting lost in any type of situation is a major threat to survival. Traditionally, getting lost can lead to confusion, anger, injury and ultimately death. In more rural survival horror locations, this can lead to creatures chasing you, or exposure, or hallucinations. However, John Erick Dowdle's 2014 alchemist horror hit *As Above, So Below* provides a new take on the sub-genre, being set in the Catacombs of Paris, where getting lost means something almost entirely different. In this film, the characters are lost in several ways, and they must strive throughout the film to overcome this.

The physical act of being lost

The first and most obvious way the film explores being lost is through the concept itself: being lost in the Parisian catacombs. With the way they twist and change, Dowdle sets the catacombs up almost as their own character, and tellingly, they play with the characters from the second they enter. Because they cannot enter by traditional means and are chased in through a hidden entrance, they are already disorientated right from the start. They are led by Papillon, an expert in illegally exploring the catacombs, however he opens their journey with the story of La Taupe, a man who lived in the catacombs and disappeared, now presumed dead. While this is framed as a cautionary tale, it also foreshadows Papillon's own fate.

The film explores the obvious tropes of getting lost first. Scarlett wants to use a map to find their way through the catacombs, while Papillon, who has been here several times before, gives an impassioned speech about not being to understand them from a map. He claims that the map cannot tell you "which tunnels are filled with water, which are collapsed in, which tunnels are evil," citing La Taupe's disappearance. "No one uses it, no one comes out." However, it is at this point where the tunnel collapses and they scramble to escape, eventually ending up in the same place they had escaped from, leading the team to turn on Papillon and his expertise.

The reason for this could be twofold. Papillon and his team are more than experienced in exploring the catacombs, and the fact they confidently bring Scarlett and her team in this way shows they usually use this entrance, further evidenced by Papillon's distinctive tag. However, this time, Papillon has not only brought inexperienced people but has then disrespected the catacombs with his comments, angering the catacombs to not only put them in danger by the tunnel collapse, but to get them to turn on him, by making his tag appear in a part of the tunnel he has previously told them is too dangerous to go down. The catacombs' reaction leads them to go down the tunnel Papillon has described as 'evil', leading them to their fate and to be further lost, an eventuality Papillon was trying to stop. It can be implied that La Taupe was able to live in the catacombs for several years until he, too, angered the catacombs, by going down the 'evil' tunnel, which led to his death and being stuck in Limbo.

Tellingly, Papillon and his team have been this way into the catacombs several times over many years, as referenced not only in the dialogue in this scene but also, as previously discussed, with scenery, however they have never descended into hell. The film implies that the entrance to hell is not the elaborate gate labelled 'Abandon all hope, ye who enter here' but is actually the hidden entrance through which they initially enter, however his team have never found themselves in this position before. It is only when they are with Scarlett, a character who is not dealing with her own personal loss and who has a goal to remove something from the catacombs, that the catacombs fight back against her, forcing the group to get lost repeatedly as a way to protect itself. This does not work for the catacombs as Scarlett is still able to remove the philosopher's stone, but by that point the catacombs have managed to trick the group into venturing further and further into its depths and through the layers of hell. Ironically, later on, Scarlett is able to use the map in someways to help them escape, but by this point, multiple people including Papillon and Souxie have died, or been 'lost' to the catacombs' wrath.

Interestingly, *As Above, So Below* utilises the setting of the Parisian catacombs, globally known as a spiralling tunnel of graves, to show how our protagonists are lost, however the themes of the text explore how each character is personally lost.

Being lost through grief
The film portrays the characters as being physically lost in the labyrinthine underground catacombs, but also explores a more subtle layer of loss by implying how the characters are individually lost to their own personal griefs, while exploring what is essentially a large graveyard. The catacombs are a memorial to loss, and each character must confront their own grief at what they have lost throughout this time. Scarlett has not recovered from the death of her father, George is haunted by the death of his brother, Souxie regrets not searching for their friend La Taupe, and Papillon was involved in the death of a man in a car fire. As a result, their losses haunt them, which then reaches physicality when they are pursued by ghosts in the catacombs.

Scarlett is the main character of the film, and it is she whose loss is most explored throughout. She is introduced as a highly intellectual woman whose path in life has been heavily guided by her father. In her introduction, she speaks about how her father had such an influence on her, how he demanded a high level of academic degrees from her, and how she now follows in his footsteps, even when the situation seems dangerous. Early in the film, she has a conversation with a contact who calls her crazy for her quest, to which she replies, "my father wasn't crazy". Her identity is so intertwined with her father's that the guilt she feels regarding his death follows her, and she is unable to unlink that grief from her own personality. She sees his ghost haunting her, not only in the catacombs but at the very beginning of the film, when she is nearly killed in an Iranian cave that is being destroyed. Scarlett is only able to achieve her goal of finding the philosopher's stone and leaving hell once she is able to say goodbye to her father and work past her grief, which is exemplified by her finding the philosopher's stone inside her. This can be seen as a representation of her finding herself again after loss, and allows her not only to complete her goals, but to save herself and those around her.

George is an interesting portrayal in that his loss is so heavily manifested within him. Initially, he does not even want to enter the catacombs out of fear of what killed his brother, and we see the child ghost of his brother Danny following him several times around the layers of hell. Later we find out that Danny drowned in a cave after George got lost trying to find help; ironically, George nearly dies in the catacombs after Scarlett gets lost whilst attempting to find the real philosopher's stone in a bid to help him. However, she does return in time to save him. While George is one of the most affected by his loss, Scarlett, who has already managed to process her grief, is able to help him atone and forgive himself, and he is able to escape.

Papillon's grief is very specific and leads to one of the more violent deaths within the catacombs. It is explained that Papillon's brother was trapped in his car when it caught fire, and Papillon let him die. Throughout the film, Papillon has been haunted by this; the man burning to death in the car is also the man seen leading Scarlett to him in the first place. It is an interesting choice on the part of the director that when Papillon is dragged into the car fire, he dies after being buried up to his ankles, with his head stuck in the sand.

The loss of Souxie can also be seen as a physical representation of a loss haunting someone. We learn midway in the film that their friend La Taupe, who lived in the catacombs, is dead, and Papillon mentions how Souxie feels guilty for not looking for him. When La Taupe eventually reappears, he is 'not normal', and speaks of how no one came looking for him. Souxie tries to confront him, but cannot take responsibility for her lack of action, or atone for her sins, and is killed by the ghost of La Taupe bashing in her head, the memory centre of the body. The grief from that loss is overwhelming for Souxie and eventually kills her.

The film's ending resolves the characters being lost in their grief. The film focuses on Scarlett, and when she is able to resolve her grief, she gains clarity as to how to leave the catacombs. She regains her true sense of self and becomes the philosopher's stone, able to lead survivors Zed and George to atone for their sins and to guide them out of their grief. It is only as they take her hands in a leap of faith that they are able to leave their loss behind and enter civilisation again.

Being lost to God
An added element to the film's themes of being lost is the strong religious aspect. Tellingly, none of the characters appear to be overtly religious, but throughout the film, several religions are referenced. The most obvious is the numerous references to God, as well as the reading that the text reflects Dante's *Divine Comedy*. There is also the fact that alchemy in the 15th and 16th centuries was linked to a religious system named Hermeticism, which considers the body of men and interaction with the material world as being against the human soul. This religion can be seen as viewing God as a magician, and is where the film's title comes from.

In Christianity, which the film appears to be closely centred around, to be sent to hell means to be separated and lost from God. This is portrayed in the film by the inclusion of a Lucifer-like figure in the deepest circle of hell; the fallen, lost angel trapped in hell forevermore. Traditionally being sent to hell means no escape, and you are lost forever. However, it is notable that our protagonists are not sent to hell, they enter of their own accord and therefore are able to escape after they atone for their sins, like the character of Dante in the *Divine Comedy*. While we do not see what happens to the characters after their return to the Above, it is implied that they will move on from languishing in their sins and improve, primarily in the case of survivor Zed, who has denied his child. They have atoned and escaped hell, meaning they have overcome and become known to God or reality again, unlike the other characters who were unable to atone and have been left behind in hell forever.

Survival horror is a wide and diverse subgenre, and allows us to explore our deepest fears in a safe environment. *As Above, So Below* enhances the viewer experience by exploring what it means to be lost threefold; physically, mentally and spiritually, emphasised by its setting of the catacombs, a memorial to loss.

Into the Wild

Losing Your Life By Choice

by Frank Schildiner

Into the Wild is a terrifying, sad, maddening tale based on the real-life death of Christopher Johnson McCandless, aka "Alexander Supertramp", in the distant wilderness of Alaska. Based on the semi-fictional book of the same name by Jon Krakauer, the tale is one that provokes a wide range of reactions, usually based on the simple fear of being lost in the unforgiving, frozen, north.

Jon Krakauer, best known for his book *Into Thin Air*, which tells a firsthand account of the 1996 Mt. Everest hiking disaster, brought the story of McCandless to the world. Later turned into a well-known, award-winning film, this story is one of the truest examples of the horrors that being trapped alone in the wilderness can invoke in one person.

Imagine, if you will, a young man climbing from a car. He is dirty, bedraggled and carrying a backpack with a rifle, fishing net and other items. He is in the deepest part of Alaska, a location called the Stampede Trail, and it is the middle of winter. The driver hands the young man, Alex, a pair of waterproof boots and tells him to call when he leaves the woods.

Alex walks into the woods, begins living off the land by killing small animals and collecting berries. He stumbles onto an abandoned bus, which an unknown person converted into living quarters, and which he dubs the Magic Bus. He cleans it up and inscribes his philosophy upon a piece of wood along with his adopted name, Alexander Supertramp.

Sounds magical, eh? However, we watch as subtle clues to his deteriorating health emerge, such as McCandless adding new holes to his belt, even as he appears somewhat content with his life as he reads Jack London, Henry David Thoreau and other philosophers and writers who spoke about nature.

The film flashes back to his early life and his conflicts prior to his quest for Alaska. Born into a wealthy family, his father is a violent bigamist, and his mother appears equally as bad. McCandless is protective of his younger sister, Carine, but despises his parents and their false life.

Graduating from Emory with high grades, McCandless rejects his parents' gift of a new car, donates his college funds to Oxfam, destroys all his identification, and sets off into the world. After his car dies in a flash flood, he adopts the name Alexander Supertramp and becomes a wanderer, hitching rides and riding railroad boxcars like a Depression-era hobo. He does not write or call his family, who are unaware that he left the world as they know it.

Along the way he meets a great many interesting people. His main topic of conversation is how the world is a terrible place and his desire for a life alone in Alaska. A kind couple named Rainey and Jan, who live on the road in their camper, grow closer to him and encourage him to live a lifestyle like theirs rather than giving up on the world. A farmer in South Dakota, Wayne Westerberg, hires McCandless for a time and suggests he learns from an outdoorsman and advises him to wait until spring before heading into the woods. A pretty teenage girl tries to have an affair with him, but he rejects the offer.

Saddest of all is a widower who lost his wife and son in a car accident while he was stationed overseas. The man takes McCandless in, shows him his craft of leatherworking, and expresses his desire to adopt the young man as a grandson. McCandless brushes him off, saying they can discuss that when he returns from Alaska, leaving the old man in tears but accepting the wanderer's choice.

We return to the wilderness where McCandless is fighting for survival while keeping a positive attitude overall. Hungry, he hunts for and shoots a moose. Although having read advice about protecting the meat and preserving it for the future, unfortunately his skills are lacking and the carcass becomes filled with maggots, ruining the remains. Later, he watches as wolves consume the pieces. In his journal, McCandless views the shooting and failure of the moose's meat as a terrible tragedy.

His life is constant work and when spring arrives, he decides it is time to return to civilization.

This is when the real danger begins. The calm stream he waded through earlier has been transformed into a violent rampaging river. He falls into the river and nearly drowns, needing to return to the bus. He then realizes that his supply of rice is rapidly dwindling and as the opportunities for fresh meat are also slim, he screams into the wilderness in frustration.

He turns to searching for berries and plants as his only sustainable food source. Slowly, his weight diminishes, his appearance becoming skeletal. His loneliness and growing starvation is exacerbated by an onset of nausea and weakness. He becomes incapable of even drinking water and is barely able to stand. Looking through his book on plants, he realizes he mistook an Alaska Pea Plant for an Alaska Potato. The former is poisonous, the latter is listed as safe.

Each day becomes a struggle even to mobilise. In a bizarre scene, a massive bear stares at him for a moment before turning away from his malnourished, weakened form. We watch as McCandless comes to the realization of the mistakes in his life. He reads Tolstoy's line "And that an unshared happiness is not happiness," before adding the words "HAPPINESS ONLY REAL WHEN SHARED".

Dying, he pens the following words:

"I HAVE HAD A HAPPY LIFE AND THANK THE LORD.
GOODBYE AND MAY GOD BLESS ALL!
CHRISTOPHER JOHNSON MCCANDLESS."

Climbing into his sleeping bag, he dreams of a tearful reunion with his parents before dying. He is alone, lost, and starving to death after having left his family two years previously without ever letting them know anything of his life. Two weeks later, moose hunters find his corpse in the Magic Bus, and a month afterwards his sister retrieves his ashes.

Into the Wild is often heralded as a biography and an adventure film. However, many such as I view this stunning work as the truest, most honest, real-life horror film in decades. Chistopher McCandless's rejection of the world and people who sought his friendship and company were sad and painful moments leading to the most terrifying monster of all, raw untamed nature. Watching a man slowly starve to death is a gut-wrenching experience, especially when so many aspects of this story were preventable.

Take the many people who sought McCandless's friendship and company. We watch as his overwhelming need for an Alaskan adventure hurts and diminishes each of them as individuals. We see the teen girl, Tracy Tatro, ably played by a young Kristen Stewart, staring into space as McCandless dreams of others, sad despite slow dancing at her prom. Or his unpleasant parents, who visibly weep and mourn his vanishing and lack of contact.

But most impacted is the narrator of the tale, his younger sister, Carine McCandless. Played with magnificent depth by Jena Malone, she fiercely loves her brother and is shattered by his lack of contact, despite their apparently close relationship.

What is left out of the narrative adds to the sheer soul-destroying horror of his unnecessary death. At the start of the film, we briefly meet a kind man who gives him a set of boots before McCandless heads off onto the Stampede Trail. This man, an electrician named Jim Gallien, played himself in the film. He offered to take McCandless into Anchorage and buy him better supplies and equipment, since the items McCandless carried were inadequate for survival. McCandless rejected the delay to his dream and left, accepting only the boots, two sandwiches, and a bag of corn chips. Gallien hoped and believed that the young traveler would return to civilization in a few days after he became hungry. Sadly, he was the last person McCandless ever saw before dying, alone and lost.

Then consider his moment at the river. According to reports, the summer glacial melting made the river impassable at the spot he had previously crossed. What McCandless did not know, because he trekked into the deepest wilderness without a map, was that a half mile from this was a method of escape. A hand-operated cable car lay a short distance from where he resided, and would have allowed him a means of returning to civilization.

There was another note that attracted the attention of the moose hunters two weeks after his death. Placed across a window of the bus it read:

"Attention Possible Visitors. S.O.S. I need your help. I am injured, near death, and too weak to hike out. I am all alone, this is no joke. In the name of God, please remain to save me. I am out collecting berries close by and shall return this evening. Thank you, Chris McCandless. August."

However, the story doesn't end with his death. The Magic Bus became something of a pilgrimage destination by those who read the many articles on his life and death. Once Jon Krakauer's book became a bestseller and was made into a film, the site became a sought-after spot despite the remote location. Rangers have had to rescue at least fifteen hikers, and there have been at least two known deaths by people trying to cross the Teklanika River that defeated McCandless. Subsequently, the Alaskan National Guard and other government agencies airlifted the Magic Bus away from the Stampede Trail. It now resides as part of an exhibit at The Museum of the North at the University of Alaska, Fairbanks.

A painful legacy, one that is hotly debated by many. Whether you believe McCandless to be a free-spirited follower of transcendentalism, or an idealistic fool who all but committed suicide due to his lack of preparation, is ultimately an individual choice based on your own view of the world. There are many articles that cover both opinions which can assist in you coming to a decision.

What ultimately results from *Into the Wild* as a film (and his life story) is a sad tale of an idealist who becomes lost in one of the densest, least forgiving environments and slowly dies before the viewer's eyes. It is a slow progression, one that is forewarned as a distinct possibility by every person who meets McCandless after he sets out on the road as a homeless traveler. They question his need for this solo journey into a location he had never visited, demonstrating that life among others who care about him would be a better fate than a life spent alone.

Emile Hirsch, as McCandless, resembles a famine victim in the last half of the film, one that even an Alaskan grizzly bear visibly rejects as unhealthy and unpleasant. From the time when he discovers the river is too high for a safe crossing, the film shows the true horror of one lost and alone, away from any form of humanity. By the time McCandless climbs into his sleeping bag, staring into the sky as he slowly dies, the viewer experiences a loss that is, in my estimation, worse than one suffered by people chased by crazed killers or monsters. Actual life can be the greatest horror anyone can experience, either on film or in reality.

Saddest of all is the simple fact that McCandless recognized his failure in the end, not simply due to his slow, painful death, but his recognition that he had rejected those who sought to warn him. As he wrote, "HAPPINESS ONLY REAL WHEN SHARED", a fact he discovered far too late.

Though there are many terrifying tales of those alone in the wilderness, I think the real-life story of Christopher McCandless, aka "Alexander Supertramp", is a horror tale that will bring true fear and pain to any viewer. Worst of all, it was preventable and will live as a powerful reminder that nature can be the most formidable of monsters in the world. As McCandless' favorite author Jack London once wrote, "Not all the monsters have fangs".

Walkabout

The Land of Lost Content

by Gary Couzens

"*This is Australia, yes? Where is Adelaide?*"

This is Church Crookham, Hampshire, England, on Monday 22 January 1979. After the nine o'clock news, my mother and I settle down to watch *Walkabout*. It was its second BBC1 broadcast and we stay until it ends around 11pm, on a school night too. *Walkabout* was the second Australian feature film I ever saw: the first was *The Overlanders*, as part of BBC2's big Ealing Studios season in 1977. There have been many more in the decades since. My Aussiephilia, and Aussiecinephilia, was already taking root.

Before it was a film, *Walkabout* was a novel, by James Vance Marshall (pseudonym of Donald Gordon Payne), first published in 1959 and originally called *The Children*. I hadn't read the novel then, but I do remember parts of it read at junior school assemblies. I was aware of the film, though hadn't seen its previous BBC showing in 1977. I was also aware to some extent of Nicolas Roeg as a director, though as I was fourteen *Walkabout* was the only one of his films up to then that I was actually old enough to see. But nothing prepared me for the shock of seeing a film the like of which I'd never seen before. After the title and the three principal actors' names come up, an electronic howl thrusts us straight into a montage, cut to extracts from Stockhausen's *Hymnen* and some didgeridoo. A young girl is at school doing voice lessons; later she walks home, running her hand along a fence, the Sydney Harbour Bridge and Opera House in the distance. A young boy, also in his school uniform, ducks home through a park. A middle-aged man, in a suit and tie, is one of many commuters on his way to work. The sequence begins with a track along a wall, giving way to a bustling street, and ends with another track along the same wall, to the desert. We are immediately confounded: who are these people and what relation do they have to each other? We are at first as lost as our principal characters will soon be. But we know we are in good hands. We have a guide.

The novel is very much a children's book, with a somewhat paternalistic late-Fifties view of its characters in its third-person omniscient narrative. It contains language which would need a flag as discriminatory nowadays. The film, scripted by Edward Bond, is not especially family-friendly, containing scenes of nudity and animal killing, including a sexual awakening perhaps fuelled by cultural taboo. This takes place in a special time away from civilisation in Australia's Red Centre, as brother and sister try to return to a home that will never be the same again.

A teenage girl (Jenny Agutter, sixteen at the time of shooting) and her younger brother (the director's son Luc Roeg, billed as "Lucien John", seven) are taken into the outback by their father (John Meillon). Roeg typically shows rather than tells, which can make his films puzzling on first viewing. But something is amiss with Father. Roeg has hinted at this already, with an Antonioni-like shot of Father sitting on a bench dwarfed by the modern architecture around him, one of them the office building where he works. But we are taken by surprise as he pulls out a gun and shoots at his children. Failing to kill them, he sets his car on fire and turns the gun on himself. The girl's first instinct is to protect her brother. They have to get home. But they are lost.

The novel differs considerably to the film. Originally, the two children were Americans, Mary and Peter, rather than seemingly transplanted Brits (played by British actors in the film, though Meillon as their father was Australian). Peter is eight, around the same age as his big-screen counterpart, but Mary is thirteen, much less so than hers. Their abandonment in the Outback is due to a plane crash and it's Adelaide they need to return to. Some of that remains in Bond's spare script – reputedly originally just fourteen pages long, when normally a page of screenplay corresponds to a minute of screen time, so Roeg had to expand it to avoid giving producers and financiers conniptions – as in the line quoted above. You may wonder why they need to return to Adelaide, as you can clearly see in the opening sequence that brother and sister live in Sydney. The attraction between the girl and their aboriginal rescuer is barely there in the novel, and his death is due to his lack of immunity to her brother's cold.

In the film none of the characters have names (in early script drafts they were Susan and Tommy), so I will use those they are given in the end credits: Girl and White Boy. Girl tries her utmost to cling on to as close a version of their normal life as possible, still wearing her school uniform, occupying herself by repeating her lessons, becoming a substitute for their mother (whom we glimpsed earlier, in their apartment). But she's aware how much peril they are in, which she tries to hide from her brother. They have to find food and water, in the baking summer sun. Roeg frequently cuts away to animals and insects scuttling across the arid ground, indifferent to the two humans passing by. The land does not welcome them. When Australia was first settled, it was declared *terra nullius*, land belonging to no one, despite the fact that it had had a civilisation for many thousands of years. It does not belong to these two children.

At this point book and film coincide. At their lowest ebb, they meet a young aboriginal boy (Black Boy in the credits, played by David Gulpilil, here spelled "Gumpilil", also sixteen at the time of shooting). Black Boy is on walkabout, something explained to us in a caption at the start of the film, added by the studio over Roeg's objections – a rare example of telling rather than showing in the whole 100 minutes. The aboriginal boy looks blankly as Girl pleads with him in English asking where they could find water, but White Boy saves the day, using the international language of mime. And so they are saved and with Black Boy's help they travel home.

Unlike them, the Black Boy is of this harsh land. For a while they can coexist with him there, as he finds water and hunts and kills animals for their food. Roeg compares and contrasts this way of the desert by intercutting with the western way of food: butchers chopping up meat, hunters shooting and gutting animals largely for sport. But there is a snake in this hot, dry Eden.

Much has been written about the cinematic gaze, the often gendered and sexualised way the camera looks at the cast through its lenses and how the audience looks at them on the screen. For much of that time, this gaze defaults to male heterosexual. Too much a discussion of gaze theory is outside the scope of this piece, but it's certainly there in *Walkabout*. Nicolas Roeg was a heterosexual man, and a director not afraid to tackle sexuality with a frankness that would not have been possible a decade earlier. With the major exception of *Performance* –

the bisexual/BDSM eroticism and gender fluidity being clearly the contribution of writer/co-director Donald Cammell – and the partial one of *The Man Who Fell to Earth* (one major character a gay man and a hint that David Bowie's Thomas Jerome Newton is bisexual), the films of Roeg's great run of the 1970s and early 1980s, one of the greatest of any British director, are all very much straight. And as their protagonists, other than those in the present film, are men, that means straight male. *Walkabout* features one of Jenny Agutter's three major teenage roles (filmed after *I Start Counting* and before *The Railway Children*, but released third of the three) and it's one point where many a teenage boy or young man developed their fandom for her. That was a fandom with a basis in eye candy, as this was the first film in which she appeared nude. Her solo lake swim late on, shot in a way to evoke Sidney Nolan paintings, is the origin of this. It's a scene of freedom, with no one in sight, of the pleasure of water against bare skin, but it's also a scene where we the audience are watching a naked girl. Roeg is much more direct about the male gaze in the short scene with a group of meteorologists, showing the attention that five men are paying to the one woman present and how clearly sexualised it is, but eroticism pervades the film. Sexual imagery abounds: Girl's first taste of the water found for them by Black Boy is via a tube and very fellatio-like, and in another scene she climbs a tree, a eucalyptus with a very vaginal cleft, her school skirt falling about her waist as she hangs upside down, her knickers on display.

And yet... Voiceover narrations and subjective camerawork notwithstanding, cinema is a third-person medium. But from time to time, Roeg takes us into the heads of both Girl and White Boy, not by voiceover but by editing: jagged cuts to memory flashbacks, superimpositions. And we're certainly in Girl's head in a scene where she talks to her brother about their aboriginal rescuer. Yes, a shirt wouldn't fit Black Boy, but why would he need one when he has a physique like he has? Jenny Agutter appears nude in the film, but David Gulpilil does too. He hadn't acted before; Roeg cast him due to his abilities as a dancer, and that no doubt contributed to his evident fitness. Girl sees his beauty, and via the camera so do we.

But if Black Boy is an object of nascent sexual desire, he's othered as well. In the original script, Black Boy's lines were written in English (with the unfortunate direction that he deliver them "in Abo") but what he speaks on screen is never translated. So if, like me, you cannot speak the dialect of Yolŋu Matha that Gulpilil uses, one of about five languages he spoke before English, you can only guess what he says. His intentions do, however, become clear. Early on, there are hints that Girl's father might harbour incestuous desires for her, and that she is aware of this to some extent, so *Walkabout* becomes a film where two men's culturally taboo attraction to a young woman, as she is becoming, lead to deaths by suicide which bookend the film. The Girl is with the Black Boy in this strange landscape, far away from the civilisation she is trying to cling on to, but much as she might desire it, she cannot join him there in sexual congress, cannot stay with him there. Civilisation still has its grip on her. This has fatal consequences.

White Boy takes this death in his stride, as he did that of his father. Despite his sister's attempts to shield him from what was happening – and her first instinct when Father started shooting was to run with him to safety – he was more aware of it than she realises. (He had noticed that Father had been drinking a lot.) But now we're in the final stretch and brother and sister find a deserted mining town with one grumpy employee to hand. But they are out of the desert and they will soon be home.

There's a theory that the children actually died in the wilderness and much of the film, from their rescue by Black Boy onwards, is a fantasy, a death dream in their last moments. But even if you don't go along with that, there is an element of dream and fantasy throughout. This comes to the fore in the closing scenes.

We're back in Sydney, seemingly in the same apartment overlooking the harbour where we started. And here is Girl, still played by Jenny Agutter but noticeably older, preparing food for dinner, wearing makeup and smoking a cigarette. Her husband returns home from work. She has now taken her mother's place, the traditional role she may well have foreseen for herself, or which had been foreseen for her all her life. Perhaps there will be children of her own in the near future.

But once it was different. Once there was a hiatus, the days and nights when she and her brother were lost in the wilderness. As her husband talks about how his day has been – nothing about how hers has been, though – her mind is elsewhere.

She, her brother and the Black Boy are back in the outback, on a sandy island in the middle of a small lake, all three of them naked, smiling, clearly happy. What was a gruelling experience, of their being lost in the desert, a time of freedom, though a freedom inextricably bound with danger, has now been suffused with the honey of nostalgia. The pain is no more, but the pleasure remains. Roeg leaves us with the words of A.E. Housman, from his poem "A Shropshire Lad", which are spoken as a voiceover before the final credits roll.

> *Into my heart an air that kills*
> *From yon far country blows:*
> *What are those blue remembered hills,*
> *What spires, what farms are those?*
>
> *That is the land of lost content,*
> *I see it shining plain,*
> *The happy highways where I went*
> *And cannot come again.*

Brightwood

You Can't Go Home Again

by John G Austin

"If you go down in the woods today, you're sure of a big surprise"
  —'The Teddy Bears' Picnic', Henry Hall and his Orchestra

"We're on a road to nowhere, Come on inside"
  —'Road to Nowhere', Talking Heads

I will freely admit that I am a sucker for any film (no matter how good or bad) which involves one or more people getting lost, whether it be in a building, in a town or city, or anywhere in the countryside. This liking is due to one simple reason, namely that I have the sense of direction of a paper plane.

This lack of a sense of direction is something inherited from both my mother's and father's sides of the family, and it normally gives me an instinctive sympathy (although this doesn't always last) with the hapless protagonists of such films. (To give my dad his due, he recognised that this was the case; unfortunately, this also resulted in my growing up with the mistaken belief that adult males would stop and ask directions when they became lost.)

For many years my favourite 'getting lost' film was the original version of *Long Weekend* (1978), with squabbling couple Peter and Marcia camping in, and not being able to find their way out of, unspoiled woodland by the sea. Since their behavior is so casually destructive of nature, my sympathies evaporated fairly quickly, and it was actually quite pleasing to see them receive their comeuppance in this great thriller.

However, being a fickle person, *Long Weekend* has now been supplanted by *Brightwood* (2022), which not only features people getting lost, but also some temporal shenanigans (another favourite in my book), some (but not excessive) gore and a memorable ending. Frankly, I think it's a damn good film.

An independent film, it was written, directed and produced by Dane Elcar (who was also responsible for cinematography, editing, sound design and camera operation). It's a lean, tense film with only two cast members, namely Dana Berger (as Jen) and Max Woertendyke (as Dan), whose normal world rapidly transitions into one of increasing anxiety, terror and (finally) horror.

And it all begins so prosaically. Dan and Jen are out for a morning jog; she is clearly angry with him, is deliberately outpacing him and also listening to a podcast about separation and divorce (the first indication that her anger with him is not just a transitory issue). He is obviously not so fit and/or suffering the effects of the previous night, whilst also attempting to get back into Jen's good graces. His remark concerning breakfast results in Jen suggesting that he could do with generating a calorie deficit rather than a calorie surplus. It also results in her suggesting/insisting that they do some laps of the local lake before indulging in some food. This is not a good decision.

And so, they take the trail which leads them to the track circling the local lake, the trail emerging by a dilapidated 'No Swimming' sign. Jen proposes that they do four laps, each at their own pace, and meet back by the sign. They separate and set off in the same direction, but each at their own pace.

And this is where things start going a bit strange. Both Dan and Jen experience some odd phenomena whilst running. Another runner comes out of nowhere and smashes into Dan, but he is not able to see who it is, and the runner is gone from sight inexplicably quickly. Both he and Jen hear a headache-inducing barrage of what seems to be multiple overlapping voices. There is also the appearance (and quick disappearance) of an individual who appears to be wearing a brown hooded sweatshirt.

Finally, when Jen completes her first lap, she discovers that the trail leading to and from the 'No Swimming' sign has vanished. What's more is that there is no indication that it was ever there; attempts to rationalise what has happened (Two 'No Swimming' signs? Someone has moved the sign? The trailhead has been covered, somehow, by leaves and branches?) show an increasing desperation to make sense of it all. They also make strenuous efforts (both separately and together) to find the trail, but without success and, when they bump into each other on their separate explorations, their conversations seem a little bit…off.

However, Dan and Jen only begin to suspect that something is really going wrong and weird when Jen drops her earbuds by the sign just before they decide, yet again, to trek around the lake. On completing the lap, they find two pairs of earbuds on the ground. Things just get worse from here on in.

So what is going on? The explanation (I think) is that the lake is both a temporal and spatial loop in which time and space behave differently. For the spatial loop the effect is quite simple: whatever way Dan and Jen decide to go through the forest in an attempt to reach 'normality', they end up right back at the lake again.

For the temporal loop, it appears that each time someone completes a lap around the lake a new 'temporal variant' or version of them is generated. However, all these versions of Dan and Jen are generated into this one reality (the lake and the surrounding forest). They exist in their own loops, but those loops can intersect with the loops of other versions of Dan and Jen.

This would also explain why Dan and Jen have had conversations with each other that don't seem quite right; they have each met versions of each other who are variants, who have had different previous conversations and experiences. (It would also explain why there are more and more earbuds on the ground each time they complete a lap and return to the sign.)

I am not going to detail any more of the events in the film; if you have seen it, then you will already know what happens. If you haven't, I don't want to spoil it (any more) for you. I will just say, however, that as the film progresses, we meet and see other versions of Dan and Jen, some of whom are still trying to find their way back home whilst meeting and interacting with variants. Others, however, appear to have given up on this and are trying to adapt to, and survive in, an environment where time doesn't pass and there doesn't seem to be any bird, animal or aquatic life around for them to eat.

So why does this film strike such a chord with me? Why have I watched it three times now (and will probably watch it again)? And what has made me recommend it wholeheartedly to friends and family? Well, there are several reasons, as discussed below.

Firstly, it is not just an episode of *The Twilight Zone* expanded to feature length. Yes, the concept could easily have formed the basis for a story in that series, but what makes it different is that the film is also an examination of a failing marriage.

Most (if not all) of us have been at a meal or a party where we have encountered a couple that manifestly hate each other. The bickering, sarcastic remarks, icy glares and uncomfortable body language result in a tangibly tense atmosphere which makes you want to be elsewhere.

Dan and Jen are this sort of couple and, as they are the only two characters in this film, it would be very easy to wish for bad things to happen to them and/or for their eventual demise. Even when they are literally going nowhere, they cannot stop the bickering, sarcastic remarks and making the sort of comments that once said, cannot be unsaid (or forgotten). It's brittle, caustic dialogue and, I suppose, might be what you would get if Mike Leigh did indeed decide to write a *Twilight Zone* episode.

Secondly, nothing (or very little) is superfluous or wasted in this film. For example, Dan and Jen repeatedly remind each other that they have been together "a long time" (and also a "stupid amount of time") and that their relationship could go in one of many "directions". Dan states that he's not much of a hunter; Jen states that she dreams of "stabbing Dan in the neck".

These choices of words are not accidental; the phraseology foreshadows that which is about to happen, or is currently happening, or will be happening. The same also applies to things that are seen in the film; not just the hooded figures, but things like tracks showing that something has been (or is being, or will be) dragged along the trail.

Thirdly, Dan and Jen are lost. They are not lost in the sense that they don't know where they are; they know exactly where they are (or think they do), but they are lost in the sense that they cannot find their way home (or, indeed, some location which would act as a starting point for finding their way home).

And this is the thing which really resonates with me, because it has happened to me on more than one occasion (albeit with happier outcomes). For example, I once had to escort a visitor from the first floor of an office building to a room on the same floor. Having delivered the visitor to the required office, I then could not find my way back to my own office. The only way I achieved it was by eventually going all the way back down to the building foyer and then finding the stairwell which led back to my office. (Okay, I had only been at work in the building for a few days, but it was still embarrassing, particularly since I kept passing by, or through, the same offices for a while, much to the increasing concern and or suspicion of their occupants.)

On another occasion, I went round the same roundabout nine (yes, nine!) times in the centre of Reading to try and identify the correct exit; I knew it was there, but I just couldn't identify it.

And lastly, in the late '80s (well before SatNav and in the infancy of mobile phones) I drove to see some friends who lived in North Wales. They had advised me that the route could be 'a bit confusing' at one point. That advice did not help me, since I ended up driving along roads forming the three sides of a roughly equilateral triangle for about an hour-and-a-half. Ninety minutes driving along the same roads, with not a house or a telephone box or a person to be seen, and with my levels of anxiety and frustration increasing proportionately at the rate at which the petrol gauge was showing the declining level of fuel in the tank. There are other occasions when this sort of thing has happened, all of which mean that I can really empathise and sympathise with Dan and Jen's predicament.

And finally, the ending to the film. Well, as it turns out, some of the versions of Dan and Jen (presumably those who have been trapped at the lake the longest (although, what does the term "longest" even mean in this situation?)) are identified as the mysterious person (or in this case, people) in the brown hooded sweatshirt (that's really just Dan's blue sweatshirt worn and caked with mud). They have also adapted the best to survive in this situation. They have achieved this by preying on other versions, not only for their clothing and shoes that they can use, but also for the sustenance they can provide. Yes, Dan and Jen are literally eating themselves to survive. Their lives have now lost any form of meaning or direction, being reduced to a very basic level of survival.

However, they are also getting along much, much better than the versions of Dan and Jen they prey upon, as shown by the shot of 'predator Dan' offering 'predator Jen' a chunk of either 'prey Dan' or 'prey Jen' and, as they sit side by side on a log by the edge of the lake whilst eating their food, she rests her head against his shoulder. It could be regarded as being a quite horrific moment of romance, or a romantic moment of horror. Either way, it makes for a great ending to a film that is both chilling and quite funny at times, as well as being very, very entertaining.

"And crawling on the planet's face,
Some insects called the human race.
Lost in time and lost in space.
And meaning."
—Richard O'Brien, *The Rocky Horror Show*

Fear and Loathing in the Arctic

by Andrew Hook

Some movies linger for reasons that initially appear unfathomable but which gradually take on substance. They tend to be those which appear with little fanfare, are low budget, and which need to be inventive because the central idea is all that they have to play with. I'm thinking here of such films as *The Borderlands* (2013, Elliot Goldner) where the dialogue-focussed relationship between Deacon and Gray dominates the film and supplies tension, but the absolute terror comes from the realisation of what they are descending into beneath the church. I'm also thinking of *Hellhole* (2022, Bartosz M. Kowalski), a Polish film that literally turns the standard demon-summoning trope on its head. The images at the conclusion of both films play repeatedly in my mind – despite having only viewed them each once – in a self-perpetuating cycle. Not to mention the final scene in John Carpenter's *Prince of Darkness* (1987) where a glimpse of continuing evil has infused my dreams and frequently has me waking with a scream in my throat.

Whilst the conclusion of *Arctic Void* (2022, Darren Mann) has been derided on many review sites (it is more cerebral than visual), it is the central concept – as with the aforementioned films – that I find most unnerving. Naturalistic acting coupled with a natural setting also impacts, and unlike many horror films where danger lies in the shadows, everything in *Arctic Void* is out in the open. And let's talk about that *open*. The film is set in an unparalleled white wilderness: the unadulterated vista of the Arctic Ocean north of the Norwegian settlement of Svalbard, and then later within the abandoned Russian coal mine of Pyramiden, where only one building on set had power and shooting exteriors required constant protection from polar bears. The knowledge that these locations are real is a major plus and the scenery is absolutely gorgeous. Cinematographer David Rush Morrison has clearly luxuriated in this, with many scenes pulling backwards from close-ups to wider views – presumably using a drone – to emphasise the isolation. To paraphrase the title of this book, there is literally *nothing out there*. Yet this metaphor isn't simply visual, but extends to the central construct itself, making the film ideal for examination within these pages.

For those who haven't seen the film, a spoiler-filled summary will be necessary. Americans Alan Mersault (Tim Griffin) and Ray Marsh (Michael Weaver) are respectively the producer and presenter of a low budget travel documentary show. They arrive at Longyearbyen airport in Svalbard with the intention of taking an Arctic Ocean boat journey to film the scenery and local wildlife. Alan is thinking of quitting the show. His wife, Mary, has become disenchanted by his globetrotting and he feels isolated from both her and their two children. He has clearly also had a battle with alcohol, resisting offers of drinks through gritted teeth. Ray is personable and slightly overbearing. He lost his sister when she was eight and he wears her necklace in memory. They therefore both arrive at Longyearbyen with some emotional baggage. Finally, with their regular cameraman having been unable to get a visa, they are joined by Sean Tibbetts (Justin Huen) who was in Norway and available at just a couple of days' notice. Sean is taciturn and evidently mysterious. Whilst on the boat he leaves a metal box on the table which Alan and Ray open. Inside is a reel-to-reel tape recorder which plays whale song. Ray has a good listen and he passes the headset to Alan, who catches a bit of the sound before Sean returns and they hurriedly pack it away.

For the moment, they are not alone on the boat. This is a tourist cruise and there are twenty of your archetypal Europeans aboard – a trio of German girls, some academic researchers, and a few couples – who are entertained by Jim (Rune Temte), a larger than life guide whose banter is on-point typical of these types of excursions. Jim is semi-Viking in appearance, and his asides about Minke whale meat tasting like human flesh hold a darker gravitas underneath his easy camaraderie.

As they journey, some hints to the plot pick up. Ray spots a seagull which appears to have no eyes, there is a conversation about geomagnetic storms which potentially can cut out power or even leave the whole Earth dark, a walrus kills her own pup, and one of those on board begins to bleed from an ear. Alan has a stomach issue from the whale meat and Ray accompanies him inside to the toilet. Sean is filming a murmuration which suddenly takes a twist and swoops. Jim is clearly puzzled by this phenomenon, but whatever happens next is out of shot. Sean says *Jesus Christ* and we pan back to a suddenly empty boat.

What I love about Tarantino's *Death Proof* are the lengthy scenes setting up who are on the face of it going to be the main protagonists, only for them all to die in the car crash instigated by Kurt Russell's stuntman character midway through the film. The interpersonal relationships of what went before are shattered and the viewer is left to start from scratch. It's an audacious move. This scene, twenty minutes into *Arctic Void*, has a similar effect, as Alan and Ray return to the deck to find the craft completely abandoned. Notebooks, phones, cameras remain onboard, but everyone – except for Sean, who subsequently emerges stating he was in the bathroom – has disappeared. As the ocean around them stretches for miles, there is no clear way that this could have logically happened. Similar to the *Mary Celeste* (which was amply provisioned when found and with her cargo of alcohol intact, with the captain's and crew's personal belongings undisturbed), the occupants have mostly vanished, albeit so quickly as to negate any sensible explanation.

Understandably, the film crew try to apply rationality to the situation, which feels like a wholly believable response. It is to the credit of director and writer Darren Mann that, unlike many stock horror characters who succumb to the usual tropes, our threesome remain relatively level headed and have reactions appropriate to the situation. All is not wholly well, though. Alan coughs blood and has an unexpected lesion on his neck. He withdraws into himself, scrolls through videos of his family on his phone, and appears shellshocked. It is Ray who spots some kind of settlement on the horizon and together with Sean manoeuvres Alan into the motorised raft (the power is out on the main boat) and they journey for help.

Where they land, however, is deserted. An old Russian mining town (genuine, as mentioned earlier) is their destination. Again, where other films might deploy standard scares like banging doors or glimpsed figures, accompanied by jarring sound effects, *Arctic Void* retains its aloofness – complemented by Nick Donnelly's perfectly scored soundtrack, which is sometimes no more than a persistent, high-pitched whine. As our protagonists wander through the abandoned buildings they realise there is little comfort beyond their meagre existence. *This is a ghost town and we are the ghosts*, says Alan. And then later, *I don't give a shit about where the people went. What I care about is why we are still here.*

This existential threat underpins *Arctic Void* with the sensation of *loss* being paramount. Alan, previously concerned about losing his family to his lifestyle, has to come to terms with *actually* losing his family through potentially losing his life. Ray becomes equally introspective, oftentimes fingering the necklace that he wears to remember his dead sister. The location itself is, of course, also lost to the world of people: an indication that we can be outlived, that structures – if nothing else – and certainly the landscape, will remain after we have gone. This sense of impermanence is wholly oppressive, and as the reasoning behind the *happening* is gradually revealed, the effect is not lessened. Despite their efforts to find additional fuel for their raft to travel further up the coast, Alan's increasing ill-health and the dichotomy of knowledge between the filmmakers and Sean indicate that there can be no escape. This is best distilled by Alan's reading of two passages in Hunter S Thompson's *Fear and Loathing in Las Vegas*:

> *Well, I thought. This is how the world works. All energy flows according to the whims of the Great Magnet. What a fool I was to defy him.*

And:

> *There is a big machine in the sky, some kind of electric snake, coming right at us. We'd be fool not to ride this strange torpedo all the way to the end. The possibility for physical and mental collapse is now very real. No sympathy for the devil. Buy the ticket, take the ride.*

There are some signs of recent life. A wounded deer in the bathrooms, a television playing static, a bowl of warm soup, a 7" record playing *The Anthem of the Soviet Union*, a bloodied polar bear which regards Alan before moving away, yet these are equally as inexplicable as the reality they are embedded in. There are no points of reference beyond the everyday, an everyday which is a façade and makes no sense.

Some understanding occurs when Alan plays a video on a small camera he pocketed when still on deck. It seems the German girls had filmed themselves tasting the whale meat, the camera held outstretched so they are all in shot. Suddenly, mid-conversation, the device falls to the floor and Sean can be seen on deck in the background, indicating that he must have borne witness to whatever occurred, rather than being in the bathrooms as he'd stated. *What are you doing here? Who are you?* Alan says. Yet the explanation begets more questions than it answers. Sean reveals he was hired to document the effects of an experiment where some kind of sonic weapon would be used to attack neural functions in the brain.

> *What did you see? What happened to those people?* Ray asks.
> *Vapourised, or something. There was this interference. My field of view shifted and when it came back, they were gone.*
> *Fuck you man. You expect me to believe this dystopian bullshit?*
> *They were just supposed to get disoriented, throw up.*
> *Quit fucking lying man, that's not possible.*
> *I don't know, man. I don't have any fucking answers. I don't wanna be here.*

Sean is exposed as a not-quite-so-innocent bystander, yet this knowledge alters nothing. The plot device is a MacGuffin. It doesn't materially change the situation. They are still isolated, Alan's physical conditioning is worsening, and whilst they have a reason for the event it remains unbelievable. Apart from Sean confirming that the use of the headphones can minimalise the effects of the experiment (hence why these three remain, but why Alan's short usage didn't amount to full immunisation and therefore explains his subsequent debilitation), there is no further science or explanation for the events in *Arctic Void*. And whilst the idea of a sonic weapon might be considered far-fetched, think on the following:

Tam Hunt and Jonathan Schooler, University of California psychology professors, have developed what they call a resonance theory of consciousness. In an article at EarthSky.org they suggest that *resonance – another word for synchronized vibrations – is at the heart of not only human consciousness but also animal consciousness and of physical reality more generally. All things in our universe are constantly in motion, vibrating. Even objects that appear to be stationary are in fact vibrating, oscillating, resonating, at various frequencies.* Whilst they suggest that *syncing-up* vibrations can facilitate emotional communication and have their feet planted firmly in the science camp, multiple religious practices – such as transcendental meditation - suggest that the universe responds to our vibrational frequency, and that we can raise our vibrations to resonate with positivity and higher consciousness. This was extrapolated into the 1993 book by James Redfield, *The Celestine Prophecy*, in which, at some point, it is written that the *ancients* reached an *energy vibration level* threshold that allowed them to cross over into a reality of pure spirituality.

If this sounds equally far-fetched, it might be worth considering the Havana Syndrome (also known as *anomalous health incidents*), which – to paraphrase from Wikipedia – is a disputed medical condition reported primarily by U.S. diplomatic, intelligence, and military officials stationed in overseas locations, where the affected individuals report an acute onset of symptoms associated with a perceived localised loud sound, followed by chronic symptoms that last for months, such as balance and cognitive problems, insomnia, and headaches. The Americans blame Cuba and Russia for this alleged sonic warfare. As they would.

Such disorientation could provide a factual reading of the events in *Arctic Void*, where skewed perceptions have led to the adoption of imagined realities. However, even if the events are to be taken at face value, the potential for them to be rooted in some kind of agreed reality is equally disconcerting. Our protagonists are not simply lost in the physical sense, but also within their minds.

It is this aspect which most intrigues me in *Arctic Void*, and which mirrors descents into self-introspection which occur in the majority of 'lost in an environment' movies. Aside from the *Twilight Zone* central idea, it is the human aspect which dwells in the memory. As a dying Alan records a message to his wife and children, as Ray removes his sister's necklace only to regain hope and replace it again, as Sean smokes a cigarette whilst walking to be *extracted* by those who conducted the experiment, we can ponder on our own attachments to reality and the truths across our lives that they may or may not contain. We can lose ourselves if we desire, but generally we find a way back unless we are in a situation totally out of our hands. An assumption of control that we impose on certain circumstances can soon be revealed as a fallacy with which to combat the chaos of our existence in this universe, but we kid ourselves not to dwell on it.

The movie concludes with Sean being shot by an unknown sniper, presumably for his filmed footage to be picked up and examined at a later date. His existence is expendable. A telephone rings in the room where Ray is waiting. Answering it would mean death. He has hope: the motorised raft now full of fuel. This is where the film ends. Some have called this an unsatisfying cliffhanger, but the resolution seems crystal clear to me. As in *Fear and Loathing in Las Vegas*:

> *The possibility for physical and mental collapse is now very real. No sympathy for the devil. Buy the ticket, take the ride.*

The perpetrators of this experiment remain anonymous. In *Arctic Void*, the horror is existentialist, nihilistic; the outcomes, personal. Reality is a societal construct. Once that rug is pulled away, we have little to fall back on. This is why *Arctic Void* lingers in my mind. Everyone eventually will disappear, even us.

Life is a Horror Movie: The Footnotes

by Ashley Stokes

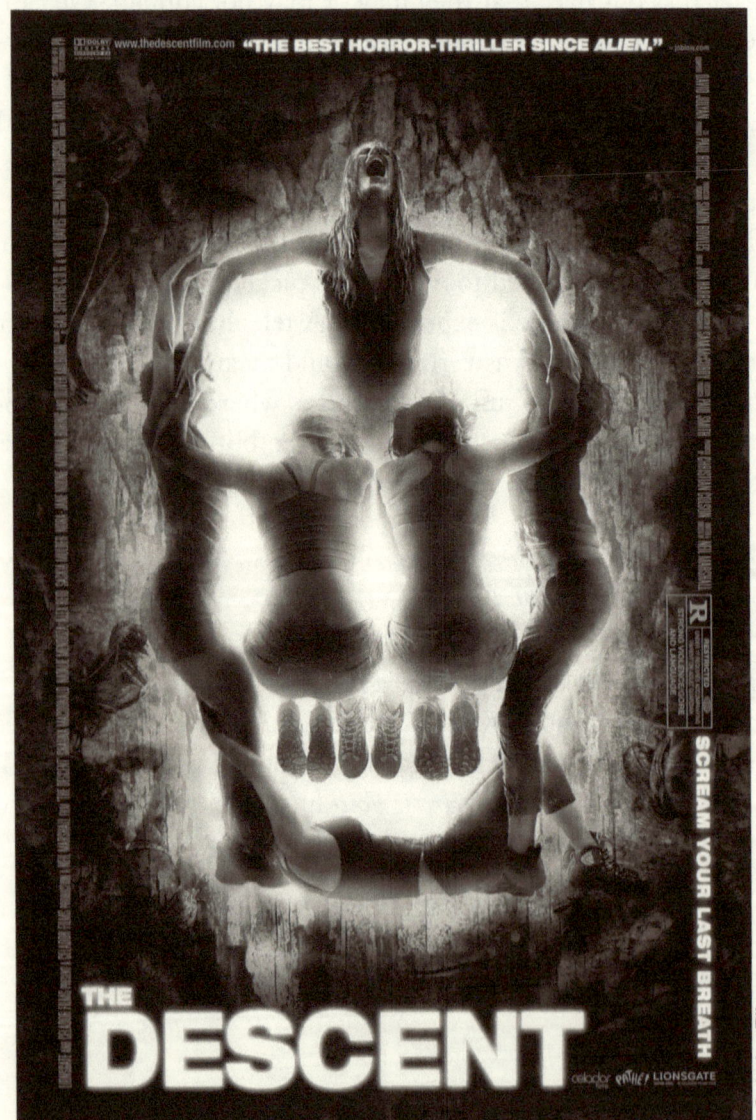

© Celador Films

Claustrophiliacs: Decoding *The Claustrophile*

The Seven Stages of Hostile Cave Exploration: *The Descent* and *The Claustrophile*, on Grief and Grieving.

This essay is reprinted verbatim from the Claustrophiliacs blog.

On this blog I am working towards critical understanding of the 1998 British found-footage horror film, *The Claustrophile*, and the vast imaginative networks and systems it opened in the minds of we few who saw and cannot forget it. In doing so I am sometimes required to shoot high and scatter the ravens that flock our moon.[1]

In last month's entry – *I Really Fucking Hope He's Kidding: Lost in the Woods with Toby Gakk* – I refuted claims made by the deceased writer Gakk in his article, *The Whisper at the Festival* (Screen Bizarre #21), that *The Claustrophile* was a major influence on the producers of *The Blair Witch Project*. Gakk saw inspiration here not just in terms of the niche-genre of both films – a revamped 90s take on the found footage trope pioneered by Shirley Clarke in her 1961 feature, *The Connection* – but in the innovative ways both properties were marketed using (supposedly, in the case of *The Claustrophile*) hoaxed support materials over traditional ads, trailers and pre-hype.

We can agree with Gakk that *Blair Witch* was a massive commercial and critical success and *The Claustrophile* a dismal failure. I will, of course, always argue that *The Claustrophile* is an artistic triumph and the *Blair Witch* three screams and a runny nose.

Of course, we must underline again that Gakk's is a false equivalence, is not substantiated anecdotally or officially, and he doesn't, or sadly never had opportunity, to fully realise the sort of film *The Claustrophile* is. We can assert with confidence that the producers and the adlibbing cast of *The Blair Witch Project* were unaware of *The Claustrophile* and could not have learned from its genius or plagiarised it in any way: they are still with us, they are all still alive.

Influence in cinematic terms is hard to prove re *The Claustrophile*. Another claim comes in one of its scant mentions in Blake Grammaticus' *The Reflective Metamorphosis: Horror in the 90s* (Routledge, 2012): 'This obscure to the point of irrelevance straight-to-video creepfest, it too with themes of grief shoddily dramatized as a visit to the underworld, no doubt prompted and prefigured 2005's more compact, coherent and admired movie, Neil Marshall's *The Descent*.'[2]

There are similarities between *The Descent* and *The Claustrophile*, true. Both films are bottle stories that feature a group of young

[1] These are not my words. They are the words of u/descender98, introvert, eidetiker, meteorologist by trade but expert on all subterranean and tunnel-based horror films, obsessive to the point of self-erasure about the 1998 British found-footage horror film *The Claustrophile*, author of the Claustrophiliacs blog and its entry *The Seven Stages of Hostile Cave Exploration*, protagonist and sole POV of my novel, *The Claustrophile*, the first draft of which was written between December 2022 and November 2023. Sometime in the autumn of 2022, I had seen a grainy, shot-with-a-potato clip on YouTube of Russian urb-exers discovering a room full of swirling and writhing roots (*The Scariest Videos EVER Captured in Tunnels* on the KingFrostmare channel). The image gave me the initial 'glimpse' that led me to want to write a story about an underground base patrolled by a creature composed of twitching roots (I know: I should be writing for *Doctor Who*, in the seventies, obviously, not now). During the Christmas vacation I decided to attempt the root creature story, giving myself a 10,000 word limit. By this time, I had already determined to write not about an underground base patrolled by a Pertwee-era rubbery dangler, but the investigation into a mysterious video that appears on Reddit from the perspective of some lone keyboard detective who thinks the Root Dangler is no hoax but a real visitation from another world. This is the point my thinking had reached in December 2022. In December 2022, too, there was nothing wrong with my mother.

[2] In February 2023, I found myself at the UK Ghost Story Festival in Derby. I ran into quite a few of my weird-fic peers and asked frequently what I was working on now. A novella, I said, about a lost British found-footage film. By this point, the discovery draft had overshot its intended wordcount but had hardly got out of the traps (welcome to my world). We were not in shortstoryville anymore. My initial intention to describe three levels of my film's underworld in 10,000 words now seemed ambitious. That the 'underground base' would have modern, medieval and cave levels implied a huge amount of world-building. Devices I'd added to speed it up only piled on more material, or gave me pacing and compression issues. The story relied on outlining and meditating upon various opinions and theories about the found-footage film, *The Claustrophile*, and thus was generating coralline, self-fructifying encrustations of film and conspiracy Lore (which was precisely how

people, all female in the case of *The Descent*, mixed boy/girl in *The Claustrophile*, forced deeper and deeper into a subterranean mantrap, an undelineated cave system in *The Descent*, something more complicated and suggestive in *The Claustrophile*, where they are hunted by hungry supernatural forces, a pack of cannibal humanoids in *The Descent*, the singularish Claustrophile in *The Claustrophile*.

Similarities, like lives, however, end.

These are fairly standard story elements in essence (on release, *The Descent* even had to jostle for popcorn with Bruce Hunt's *The Cave*, which although inferior, has the same plot template: down they go, down they stay).

It's not difficult to imagine, as with *Blair Witch*, that the makers of *The Descent* could have assembled its parts without reference to *The Claustrophile*. However, is it possible to substantiate that both films see cave exploration as metaphors for grief and grieving?

Grief, according to the Swiss-American psychiatrist Elisabeth Kübler-Ross, is processed in Seven Stages: Shock/Denial, Pain, Anger, Depression, Upward Turn, Reconstruction and Acceptance.[3]

In *The Descent*, the first five minutes work extremely hard to establish grief as a theme. By the time the title appears, we are in no doubt that we have plunged into the hole that grief dug.

On 3 minutes, Sarah Carter is joyfully rafting rapids with her thrill-seeking frenemy Juno. On the drive home, husband Paul glazes over and loses control of the car (Sarah's last words to him are, 'You seem a bit distant'). The car is hit by a builder's truck loaded with copper pipes that smash through the windscreen and spear both Paul and young daughter, Jess. A third-minute child impalement is certainly SHOCK.

When Sarah comes out of SHOCK in hospital, reality seems to be vanishing, shutting down. When Sarah is chased by needy swathes of darkness, her running is a manifestation of DENIAL. She is unable to embrace the darkness, submit to darkness.

Once Beth – the good friend – finds Sarah in the hospital corridor, she has to calm her down from her ANGER at cruel reality. Sarah is left only with the PAIN of a world now recalibrated by absences and hellish grief.

my Surrey gigantopithecus story developed from an intended 8,000 words story into the novel, *Gigantic*). By now, I had two parallel storylines: the plot of the film, and Descender's expedition into the 'set' of the film. I had fleshed out and vocalised the members of the Reddit group r/eerie-england who had only previously appeared as a broad-brush entity in my story *The Hinwick Effigy*. Descender had a flat share nightmare/lost-love issue in his backstory and was directing the story at another person, the identity and significance of who I did not yet know. I'd also given Descender an eidetic (ie, photographic) memory so he can't forget the film no one else alive can remember. Into this mix, at random, I gave his memory complicating factors. Firstly, an adoptee, he doesn't know who he is and can't recall his early childhood or real parents. Secondly, he has only two flashes of unaccounted for childhood memories: being shut out of a cattle shed (some sort of turmoil inside); and standing at the top of a long dark staircase leading down into a black cellar, some sense that we are going to have to go down despite an interdiction, no idea what is down there, could be Nyarlathotep, could be Eamon Holmes. There is plenty to work towards, therefore, plenty of questions to answer, and I like the story-so-far, it feels urgent, magnetic; writing it is like being in a trance. Down. There is always more down. Around this time, during a routine phone catch-up, my mother tells me she is seeing the doctor as she might have a bladder infection.

[3] By May 2023, I have now reached the complex sequence in the story I call The Chapel of the Infinite, one of its longer stretches where a lot happens in both timelines. I have now written approximately 44,000 words, around 140 pages. We have taken the last flight out of Novella. We have gone on holiday by mistake, and we are now writing a novel. Down and down we go. I have also worked on what is at the bottom of the cellar stairs. Descender's mother is dead in the dark at the bottom of the stairs. I throw this in quite casually. I still don't know who she is or why she is down there. Has she been jump-scared by Nyarlathotep or Eamon Holmes? Has she had a cardiac arrest? Consumed by mutant rats? Don't know, and I won't until I write the penultimate sequence. All I know is that Child Descender still doesn't want to go down there. So far, I have used the cellar steps image to reiterate the blocks and oddities in his memory. As the main story thruline progresses,

Thus in the first ten minutes, Sarah Carter has already cycled through SHOCK/DENIAL, PAIN and ANGER, leaving the overwhelming bulk of the run-time to explore her DEPRESSION.

At 6 minutes, time has passed since the accident. Beth's Jeep glides through thick pine trees. In the passenger seat, Sarah looks obviously depressed and not at peace, something Beth must notice as she asks Sarah if she wants to turn back from what we realise is an adventure holiday organised by Juno, a meet-up with old, we assume university, friends with a history of sporty bonding activities behind them.

Despite the frivolity and girls-behaving-badly atmosphere of the evening reunion at the cabin, where we meet the others (Juno, Holly, Sam and Becca), Sarah can't sleep afterwards and has a nightmare about being impaled. She also necks pills we assume are antidepressants.

Once the women have lowered themselves into the cave, Sarah's existential struggle begins, as marked by the rather gothic trope of a release of bats. Juno announces that, 'there is only one way out of the chamber and that's down the pipe'. The pipe is a tight crack in the rock. Glimmering daylight fades into the distance above. The indifferent environment becomes the manifestation of grief.

In one of the key scenes in the film, at 31 minutes, Sarah gets stuck in a tunnel. Beth, the good friend, goes back for her and repeatedly asks a panicking Sarah what she is afraid of. Sarah keeps shouting that she is stuck, suggesting she has capitulated, is stopperred forever with no way out of her grief. Beth tells her that the worst thing has already happened, which begs the question: when the worst thing has already happened, what is left for us? [4]

At the first major plot point, Sarah does just-about escape the now collapsing tunnel, but there is only more down into an abyss. This is quickly followed by thematic development and plot-ratchetting devices: Sarah has a vision of Jess blowing out her birthday candles; Juno admits she has lured the women into an unmapped cave to recapture their receding youthful bravado; Sarah sees something in the cave. When this is confirmed as a Crawler (a devolved, cannibalistic troglodyte) at 47 minutes, the until-now psychological-person-versus-nature vibe of the film morphs into proper supernatural horror. Grief as he ventures deeper and deeper under the ground, this memory, and that of the cattle-shed door will reformulate, recover. He will start to remember taking the steps down one by one, terrified and fighting his little-boy fear. As the novel's central journey continues, so can this trip down the stairs to darkness and death. In my notebook entry of 28th April 2023, in a sketch for a scene where the adult Descender reaches a vast rock stairwell heading even further down into the earth when he is already hundreds of meters beneath the surface, I have written, 'OPENING LINE - I know who is at the bottom of the cellar stairs but I do not know who is at the bottom of the cellar stairs'. Back in Sutton, during these last three months, my mother has been unsuccessfully treated for the bladder infection. A course of antibiotics has had no effect. Whatever the discomfort is, it is still bothering her. She is feeling tired, but she is 78. A series of exploratory hospital tests reveal her discomfort is caused by unaccountable lesions on her spleen. There are cells in her spleen, too, that her doctor does not like, but he's convinced they are not cancerous. At the end of May, she is scheduled to have her spleen removed as a precaution. Even though the procedure is straightforward, the events surrounding it prove fraught. The operation is to take place at 7am at a hospital a long drive from my parents' home. They stay overnight at a pub. The following morning, as my father, who is 82, tries to leave, a condition he has with his leg, something he has no doubt put-off addressing as my mother has been ill, becomes chronic and, wracked with agony, he can hardly walk. Rather than return to the hospital, he drives home in blinding pain, on motorways, in traffic, which takes him three hours and at the end of the ordeal he is too weak to get out of the car. The following day, a landline glitch means the home phone does not ring but sounds engaged to the caller. Various family members, including my recuperating mother panic when the phone goes unanswered and no one knows where my father is. He is at home, of course, just oblivious. At this time, there are eerie premonitions, fear and catastrophising as the reliably contactable become uncontactable, wink out of sight, and the beat of time, in its very slowness feels hideously rapid and bearing-down as it now seems to have been bearing-down for all of my 53 years. To cut a long story short, not long after my mother has her spleen removed, my father has an operation to unblock an embolism on his aorta. When I visit them on the 27th of May, she looks remarkably well despite has either broken reality, or life is a horror movie. By 54 minutes, when all of the women see the Crawlers, we can assume, our genre-awareness kicking in, that each will be picked off in turn to exacerbate Sarah's isolation and lone struggle.

What now follows is a pell-mell plummet through an infernal maze as plot-tension escalates. Holly is murdered by Crawlers. Juno mortally wounds Beth. Sam is killed. Becca dies at the next beat. Sarah realises Juno was having an affair with Paul, hence his distance and not attending to the road that got Jess killed. This also makes sense of what Juno meant earlier when she'd said she too lost something in the accident, and the significance of her saying, when she and Sarah had been the last to cross a gaping chasm at 37 minutes, 'it's about going back to who we used to be.'

Nadir-DEPRESSION, the bottom, comes at 1:25, when blood-streaked, mad-eyed and in mortal combat with Crawlers, Sarah is palpably not the same character she was at the outset. She is now whittled-down like a flint axe-head, a killer stripped of her motherhood and humanity, but no longer haunted.

We can therefore see the UPWARD TURN in the successive beats of Sarah ridding herself of her shadow, Juno, and discovering, at 1:27, a sloping tunnel leading to the surface and daylight.

At 1:28, RECONSTRUCTION comes with a prospect of future happiness and a rapturous break-out into sunshine. When Sarah finds the Jeep, she drives with freedom and abandon, mirroring her domination of the rapids during the opening shot, except now she is free of Juno, her betrayer. At 1:29 she pulls up and sobs in a release of emotion before physically purging. Then she sees a spectral Juno in the car. The ghost here signifies this is a dream sequence. There is no release, nothing to RECONSTRUCT. [5]

The cave still wants her.

Bleakly, then, we find ACCEPTANCE at 1:30 when Sarah revives in a bone pit. She sees Jess again blowing out her birthday candles. She now accepts Jess is dead. She now accepts that she too is dead. This is not tragic. It is cathartic. She has found comfort in her memories of her daughter. Had she escaped, there would only be a world of ghosts being sore and the distress she has been put through. My father looks ashen, shaken, frail. The whole thing has been sobering for me and my brother: parents not just getting, but being old; parents losing control of themselves. Still, both operations have been a success. It still does not feel like the next step down into the cellar when my mother tells me that cancerous cells have been found in her spleen, but the doctors are very sure the cancer has not spread, that they caught it in time, whatever it is.

[4] In *The Claustrophile*, I write: *I am at the top of the cellar steps, I remember being at the top of the cellar steps and the smell of wrong and the deep drops between wooden step and wooden step, floating dust specks that glitter in the beam of light that slants in through the kitchen window behind me and beyond this, the frontier of my special memory – I shift my concentration from keeping my eyes shut and trying to repress my lungs, attempting to suck all of me into my navel, into my birthing, to shrink me – it slithers and hisses and at the top of the cellar steps, I turn my back to the light, let my first foot fall, then my second and start to crawl backwards into the cellar, down into the smell of wrong. I have never been this far before. I have never come this far down.* For Descender, then, things are beginning to shift. I write this sort of passage, I am so deep in my trance-state, my determination to make a cathedral of words, meanwhile seeing no connection with the actual series of alarming conversations I have with my mother in June and July. After each, to stay sane, to remain stoical, I can only conclude we know nothing and no one knows anything anyway, these things being inscrutable, interpretations open, words hedge, medical jargon, legalese etc. All can be interpreted as no one knows anything until we know everything. Even so, all news is bleak. Firstly, the hope the cancer had not spread was unfounded. There's a tumour in her liver. Then my mother rings me on a Saturday morning while am sitting in my dressing gown writing about tunnels. She tells me the cancer is terminal. She is distraught. She is sorry. I am distraught. I am sorry. None of us knows yet what this means, though. I know from presently workshopping a cancer survivor's memoir that 'terminal' can mean you die with it, but not of it, and by cultural-osmosis that cancers can be slowed to a crawl. She sends me a copy of the hospital report. The cancer is called angiosarcoma (which sounds fucking horrible, like something evil that lurks in the darkness, Lovecraftian, tentacular,

and a need to keep running from her trauma. She now has nothing to lose, nothing to fight. She has found balance, though. She has found peace.[6]

We'll set aside any discussion here of the film having different endings in different territories (and a meritless sequel), but *The Descent* does have other themes. It is also a story of the transit of thrilling youth into adulting and its discontents (as Sam says to Beth in the revels at the cabin scene, 'I hear it all starts to fall apart at twenty-five'); human insignificance versus brute nature as symbolised by the sacrifice of human females to papier-mâché cave walls; of the treachery and magic of friendship; how things disappear as we age; and, apt in a part-psychological horror, a questioning of reality and unreality and their shades and intersections; but just like its tunnels and chambers vex and trap us, it is hard to give the slip to the feeling *The Descent* is finally a bleak, neat and very Englishly unflinching discourse on grief as dead-end.

Compare this with *The Claustrophile*, where things are rarely lucid and thematically undecided. Everything is unstable from the off. Environments warp and taper. Time breaks. Screenplay grammar is stretched to the point of collapse. There is only one oblique ending, yet the set appears to extend beyond the final beat into infinity, endlesssness. If the camera would only keep running, we would see forever …

At the outset, the Snyder Party announce only their intention to explore a legendary underground complex they claim to have uncovered. All is rather playful and the only hint of conflict is that Hazel and Jinx perhaps think the most articulate of the group, Bridget, is eccentric, hippy or weird. This isn't unimportant, but it is not heavily flagged. That there is something love-triangular between Snyder, Skeet and Bridget is present but not said. The characters have no backstory that springs into relevance once the underworld levers its pressure and springs its surprises. It's only in the Chapel of the Infinite scene, in Skeet's Incantatory Rant, do we get any sense of shared history at all. Unlike *The Descent*, though, little is provided by camerawork and expression. Contingency follows contingency. Unlike the established cunning, dripping-wet). Both rare and aggressive, it attacks the linings of the veins and lymph vessels. Doctor Google tells me there is a 30% probability of treatment of angiosarcoma extending life by five years. I don't like these odds. I don't like five years. On the other hand, they are just statistics, only morons trust Doctor Google, and my mother has signed up for a revolutionary trial, something that targets only the cancer cells, not the surrounding tissue. I read that Andy Taylor, guitarist with Duran Duran has been treated for stage 4 prostate cancer with what sounds like a similar new medical procedure, and although he was not expected to live is now 'asymptomatic' and back on the road. I play *Last Chance on the Stairway* and convince myself no one knows anything yet. People go on for years. People persist, manage. End-of-life can trickle on endlessly. Nothing is certain. We will have years to prepare. The trial, which involves conventional chemotherapy as well will take us up to February 2024. This now seems like a vast parenthesis in which all eerie whispers can be banished into the background and fingers kept crossed. Not that there are no other ominous life-moments. My brother and I agree to take power of attorney over our parents, given their health situations and the events surrounding my mother's operation. This feels heavy. This feels sad, an inversion of order. In early August, I travel down from Norwich again. We are to sign attorney papers with witnesses. En route, I meet an old university friend of mine who is over from Canada, where he now lives. He has known my parents since the eighties. I had intimated to him on Skype that this might be the last time he sees her. We take the train from Victoria. We arrive. It is a summer's day, quite beautiful. She is in her element, sociable, pleased to see everyone, making lunch. My brother is there, and an old friend of my mother who will act as the witness. You would not think my mother was in her seventies, let alone is terminally ill. She is robust, healthy, fun. It feels a bit like a party. We sign documents. We drink. We laugh. Take photos. At some point in the afternoon, my father tells my brother that the cancer trial paperwork states she is expected to die within a year. Something stares back at us from the bottom of the stairs.

---

[5] On page 166 of *The Claustrophile*, I write, obliviously, unself-reflexively, *solitude protects me from what is at the foot of the cellar stairs*. This smacks me with nothing beyond its meaning for Descender, who I do not confuse with

actors in *The Descent*, the unknown cast of *The Claustrophile* do not appear to be acting and their performance has been described by Grammaticus, Gakk and others as 'shit'. However, they are not, in my opinion, actors, or acting.

Perhaps the main difference is that in *The Descent* we know why, on a human level, we are going down. *The Claustrophile* never favours its audience in this way. There is no why. As Skeet says before the horrors of the Birth Canal sequence begin, there is only more down. There is only darkness. There is only claustrophobia, the crush. Only madness, the dream. There is shock and loss, but no time to grieve. There is no one to grieve, no one to grieve the Snyder Party but me.

Grammaticus is right that *The Descent* is a feature film thematically underpinned with ideas about grief that are not at all comforting.

The Claustrophile is not even a film, though. It's a disjointed fly-on-the-wall documentary, part snuff movie, part cosmic revelation. The only way Grammaticus could come to the conclusion the films echo is if he has never seen *The Claustrophile* and his sole resource has been this blog, cribbing from me and connecting the wrong stars to create a sham constellation and pat conclusions.

Of course, he has not seen *The Claustrophile*.

It's not only that he clearly doesn't understand it. He does – as far as I know – still walk this earth to write to his deadlines, crack jokes, spin lies. [7]

myself, who is not my mascot, my catspaw. In retrospect, the summer and autumn of 2023 have a strange surreal sedateness and phoney-war calm. It is agreed that we can't visit our mother while she is undergoing the trial. The thinking is that her metabolism is so weakened by both the cancer and the chemo and related treatments that passing on the gentlest of colds might overwhelm her already stressed immune system. Assuming I will not see her until February, I try to stay in regular contact. I call when I can, but it is hard to judge how things are, only that things are not good. I know what chemo does to people and I know she will find it humiliating. I do not want her to suffer it. Over the summer, I write every day about tunnels and there being more down. I moonlight on short fiction at weekends. In mid-August I visit my girlfriend in Malmö and we go on a road trip to Stockholm, Sigtuna and Uppsala. I send my mother photos to show her I am happy and she must not worry about me on top of everything else. I am staying in a town founded by Odin. I have had coffee with one of Sweden's top horror writers. I am living my best life. In September, Eygló and I attend Fantasycon in Birmingham, where we are busy with readings and panels and talking shop. We read *Play Voidal for Me*, a collaborative story, together at a Stories in the Dark event organised by Kit Power, then listen to him read an extract from his beautifully heartfelt and honest lifewriting about witnessing his father's death and the encouragement his father had given him in his own adventures in fiction and criticism. I have a sobering feeling that I could not write as head-on and as honestly as this, being too tricksy, all flow, rhythm and clatter. I live in these rabbit holes. I displace, refract, haunt. I am not a worthy subject. I am not a reliable narrator. I am a shrug. I tell other people's stories, people who do not exist, that I assemble from snippets and parts, dice rolls, cut-ups. It does not strike me that I may one day have to journey to where Kit has returned from. It does not strike me that I may one day want to, need to. In the autumn, I enter deep into the endgame of *The Claustrophile*. It's now a 100,000 word wyrd white worm, as English as perverting the course of justice, esoteric, uncanny and strange, my magnificent downward death-spiral and doom loop, my *House of Leaves*, my pyramid. My notebook entry on November 7th contains a boxed note of the Seven Stages of Grief, a reference to help me describe Descender's thought-processes and associations at the plot's resolution. This is for him,

not me. I am the dimmest reader of myself. Like you do, at this time I write a side-story called *Dimmer* about an entity that lurks in a bottomless lake. This is what people do. This is how people continue. Down, down, bottomless, bottomless. One morning in November my mother rings me and tells me there is good news. The tumour in her liver is over 20% smaller. Some hours later my father calls in a distressed state. She is being taken off the miracle trial. They are talking about palliative care. Later, I understand that although the tumour had shrunk, seven more were found in her liver. The cancer had also spread to her spine. Any hope the trial would produce some Andy Taylor outcome is dashed.

6 On the 24th of November I finish *The Claustrophile*. My brother and I visit my mother, who we have not seen for months. She has said she wants to talk about her affairs, though in the end she seems to have little to add to what we already knew. She is thinner and wears a headwrap as her hair has fallen out. It is hard to see this. She hates it. We stay a few hours. I give her two books I have stories in, one with a big fuck-off picture of King Kong on the jacket. I tell her it's every little boy's dream to one day feature in a book with a big fuck-off picture of King Kong on the jacket. She says, 'It's a bit weird, Ashley'. This is the last thing she ever says about my writing. We have questions, but no one asks them. No one mentions Christmas, so I decide I will be in the way if I invite myself. Before Christmas I go to Krakow with Eygló, where I get COVID after one day and spend most of the break watching Netflix in the Air B 'n' B. When I come back, the *Claustrophile* draft is sent out to beta readers. The day before Christmas Eve, I fly to Sweden and spend Christmas with Eygló. I cook Christmas dinner because the Swedes know bugger-fuck-all about how to make a Christmas dinner. I introduce pigs-in-blankets and sage stuffing to Scandinavia. I call my mother and wish her a happy Christmas. She sounds OK. She speaks to Eygló for the only time. Eygló tells her I am a good cook. Mum says she knows that. She thanks Eygló for looking after me. I do not realise the significance of this until later and when I do, it hurts. The business of the cellar steps does now begin to chime and bother me and I worry that I should take them out of *The Claustrophile*, or abandon *The Claustrophile* altogether. The dead mother at the bottom of the stairs. I would not have written this had I known. I did not

feed off her. I did not make this happen, tempt fate. I did not. I tell myself I did not. I am not in control. I do not calculate. I saw only what I saw in my mind's eye. The Descender is not real. The mother at the bottom of the stairs is not my mother. When I return from Sweden, I feel the need to see my mother urgently. My father seems to want to put off a visit. He thinks she is not up to it. She has taken to her bed. My brother, my nephew and myself finally make the journey again on January 12th. She is in bed when we arrive and looks far more stricken than six weeks ago. She is yellowing and it takes her considerable time and effort to get down the stairs even with help. I hold her hand on the sofa. I show her some photos of Krakow and Malmö. I don't know what else to do. She seems serene and says she has no problems with anyone. She says she has had a good life. Her main wish is not to die in hospital. The morphine and the cancer make it hard to concentrate, she tells me. When she becomes too tired and wants to go back upstairs, the three of us leave. I assume I will see her again soon. I will need to come more regularly. I have a grim feeling she does not have another year in her. Six days later, on the morning of January 18th, I am writing about an alien mould that absorbs memories, just as a real live human being spends his time, when my father calls. She has passed, in her sleep, in her own bed, sometime in the night. We have all stepped off the bottom stair.

[7] Once we have left the bottom stair behind us and we are out on the cellar floor, on one of the mornings following her passing, because he seems unaware of the concept, I tell my father, hidebound by cliche, that grief is a process. Some say it has five stages. Some say it has seven. I don't add, according to Descender98's analysis of parallels between 2004 psychological horror *The Descent* and the 1998 British found-footage horror film, *The Claustrophile*, it has seven stages. He asks me what stage he is at. I tell him I don't think it's like that. You can't plot it on a graph. You can't time it like a boiling egg. I realise I know nothing about grief, only that my grief is different to his and unlike the grief of anyone else. Like the ghost in Hill House, I tell myself, where I walk, I walk alone. People are kind, though. I am not alone. I am alone. I am always telling myself that where I walk I walk alone anyway. I have not grieved before. I know nothing of the grieving process, only the creative process: jagged, inscrutable, semi-random, dogged,

mystical, disorderly, non-chronological, simultaneous, oblique. In films, in stories, I see people explode in rage or pain, see characters sit for hours, brooding in darkened rooms, or get wankered on booze or drugs, start fights in bars, take it out on bystanders, wail at God's darkness, sell souls, make bargains. I expect it to all hit me at once, like an atom bomb, like cosmic horror. I knew she was dying but I did not expect her to die. I was not ready. She was ready. I was not ready. I have my moments. On my first return to Norwich, I break down in public on a replacement bus service parked outside Newbury Park Central Line station as I post a message on Instagram and Facebook letting people know my mother has passed accompanied by a photo of the two of us at my graduation. I post this in part because she died two days before my birthday and it's hard to keep receiving messages wishing me a great day. Otherwise, I feel I have been swallowed by an abyss. I am cold. I hear voices. I have an odd dream back in my flat where a tall shadow figure taps me on the shoulder and says, 'Ashley, it's time.' In the void of me, nothing is quite real anymore. The funeral is booked for the end of February. It is a long time to wait. Writing and reading the tribute at the funeral seem to me to be the least I can do. My father and brother don't want to do it; I'd rather I did it than the celebrant; if I were a carpenter I'd make the coffin; if I were a florist I'd make the wreath. Writing the Tribute is easy and takes 15 minutes. Compiling and collating, planning and forming it is impossible and takes my whole life. I have always had a strange relationship with time, ever since I spent six months in hospital when I was eleven, two and a half of those months in a full-body plaster case that meant I could not even sit up. I have always known that *soon* it will pass and I will not be like this. *Soon* I will be out of the cast. *Soon* I will be a proper writer. *Soon* decades will have gone and I will be old and I will be reading at my mother's funeral. This is the hardest thing I have ever done. I would rather have another bone graft. We were together throughout that. I have put a kind of comic interlude in the middle of the tribute to make the passage easier to read, to distract me from what I am saying when I read it aloud. The day comes forward in shudders and shunts, visits to tailors, more train journeys, the putting on of unfamiliar clothes, a ride in a car following a hearse through streets I have been running away from all my life. The surreal void feeling crashes when we arrive at the crematorium chapel and the music my father has selected is

playing. I somehow manage to hold my inner line and not weep. I stand up and read and do my best and this is not enough but it suffices. At the Wake, the PowerPoint presentation my brother has put together, photographs from across the span of her life, some black and white, some in colour, not in any chronology or order, unthemed, untitled, hurts me more than anything, this is what life is like, this is what grief is like, and in this I realise and I hurt. In *The Descent*, it is sometimes said that the true horror lies not in the hostile cave and its cannibal troglodytes, but in the suddenness with which Sarah's life is ruined by the car accident at 3 minutes. In *The Claustrophile*, I hope the true horror is in the not-knowing what to believe. I don't know. It's all the same difference and indifference, time shuffling its pack. My mother was alive and seven months later she was not. I feel inadequate. I have lost my voice. I hear her voice. I feel her watching me, in the kitchen, at the door. I cannot say more. This is about me, but it shouldn't be, but where things should be as they should, I do not know where to begin. I am Ashley James Stokes, the name that she gave me. These are my words.

Recommended Viewing

Arctic Void (Darren Mann, 2022)
As Above, So Below (John Erick Dowdle, 2014)
Backcountry (Adam McDonald, 2014)
The Blair Witch Project (Daniel Myrick & Eduardo Sánchez, 1999)
Bone Tomahawk (S. Craig Zahler, 2015)
Brightwood (Dane Elcar, 2022)
Bring Out the Fear (Richard Waters, 2021)
Calibre (Matt Palmer, 2018)
Calvaire (Fabrice du Welz, 2004)
Cannibal Holocaust (Ruggero Deodato, 1980)
Cold Ground (Fabien Delage, 2017)
Dead End (Jean-Baptiste Andrea & Fabrice Canepa, 2003)
Deliverance (John Boorman, 1972)
The Descent (Neil Marshall, 2005)
Event Horizon (Paul W.S. Anderson, 1997)
Fortress (Stuart Gordon, 1992)
The Hills Have Eyes (Wes Craven, 1977)
In Fear (Jeremy Lovering, 2013)
Into the Wild (Sean Penn, 2007)
Long Weekend (Colin Eggleston, 1978)
Meek's Cutoff (Kelly Reichardt, 2010)
Ravenous (Antonia Bird, 1999)
The Ritual (David Bruckner, 2017)
Rituals (Peter Carter, 1977)
The Ruins (Carter Smith, 2008)
Swiss Army Man (Daniel Kwan & Daniel Scheinert, 2016)
The Texas Chain Saw Massacre (Tobe Hooper, 1974)
Time Trap (Mark Dennis & Ben Foster, 2017)
The Tunnel (Carloi Ledesma, 2011)
Wake in Fright (Ted Kotcheff, 1971)
Walkabout (Nicolas Roeg, 1971)
Wolf Creek (Greg McLean, 2005)
Wrong Turn (Rob Schmidt, 2003)
YellowBrickRoad (Jesse Holland & Andy Mitton, 2010)

About the Authors

About the Authors

John G Austin was born in London. A retired safety professional, he lives in Hampshire with his 'absolute goddess' (her term, not his!) of a wife (Dee) and a small ginger dog (Bella). A self-confessed comic book nerd and a fan of horror and the supernatural in all forms of media for over fifty years, "Brightwood: You Can't Go Home Again" is his first published piece.

Gary Couzens has had articles, film and book reviews published in *Black Static*, *ParSec*, *Interzone Digital* and *Roads Less Travelled*, *Cine Outsider* and *The Digital Fix*, with a particular specialist interest in Australian cinema. Gary's fiction has been in *F & SF*, *Interzone*, *Black Static*, *Midnight Street*, *Roadworks* and other magazines and anthologies, as well as the collections *Second Contact and Other Stories* (Elastic Press, 2003) and *Out Stack and Other Places* (Midnight Street Press, 2015).

Dan Coxon has won two British Fantasy Awards, for *Writing the Uncanny* and *Writing the Future* (both co-edited with Richard V. Hirst), and has been shortlisted for the awards a total of seven times. He has also won a Saboteur Award, and was a finalist for the Shirley Jackson Awards. His short stories have appeared in various anthologies and magazines, including *Shakespeare Unleashed*, *Beyond the Veil*, *Fiends in the Furrows III* and *Great British Horror 7: Major Arcana*. His most recent anthology is *Heartwood: A Mythago Wood Anthology* (PS Publishing).

Daragh Fleming (author of *A Brief Inhalation* and *Lonely Boy*) is a writer from Cork, Ireland. He has work appearing in several literary magazines including *Southword*, *Crannóg*, *Stand*, *Gutter*, and more. He was highly commended for both the Patrick Kavanagh Award and the Fool for Poetry Prize in 2023, and shortlisted for the Alpine Fellowship Poetry Prize in 2024. He won the From the Well Competition in 2021 and the Ducairn Flash Competition in 2024. Daragh was also shortlisted for two Mental Health Media Award for his TEDx Talk on using creativity to enhance and maintain our mental health.

Jason Gould is a writer of fiction, non-fiction, and script for stage and screen. His work has appeared in *At the Lighthouse* and *Humanagerie* (Eibonvale Press), *Port* (Dunlin Press), *A Shadow Within: Evil in Fantasy and Science Fiction* (Luna Press), *Structo*, *Black Static*, and the *Terror Tales* series (Telos Publishing). He holds a Creative Writing degree from the University of Hull, and won the *Dead Pretty City* crime writing competition in 2017.

Adam Groves got lost in the unruly realm of cinema sectarianism back in 1996, when his writings on film were initially published. Some claim he has yet to be found. Whatever the case, Adam strongly recommends you read his reviews, reflections and ramblings in TheBedlamFiles.com, *Shock Cinema*, *Weird Fiction Review* and Kurodahan.com, and that you watch plenty of Ozploitation movies (because truly, one can never get enough).

Andrew Hook has had over a hundred and eighty short stories published, with several novels, novellas and collections also in print. Recent books include a time travel novel, *Secondhand Daylight*, written in collaboration with Eugen Bacon (2023, Cosmic Egg Publishing), and *Commercial Book* (Psychofon Records): a collection of forty stories of exactly one thousand words in length inspired by the songs from the 1980 record *Commercial Album* by The Residents. His non-fiction book about the movie *Union City* should appear from the Electric Dreamhouse imprint of PS Publishing later this year. andrew-hook.com

Gaynor Jones is a writer, carer and horror fan based in Oldham. She is the recipient of a Northern Writer's Award for her (unpublished) short story collection, *Girls Who Get Taken*. She is a frequent performer at spoken word nights and was a guest of *For Books' Sake* at the 2019 Edinburgh Fringe. She has won several writing competitions and has taught for Comma Press and Didsbury Arts Festival among others. In 2024 she was a virtual writer-in-residence for Melbourne UNESCO City of Literature. She is represented by Laura Williams at Greene & Heaton. www.jonzeywriter.com

About the Authors

Lisa Moore-Smith wrote *Azeman: the Testament of Quincey Morris* (Black Shuck Books), proud finalist for a 2022 Shirley Jackson Award. A grim tale of hers appeared in the 2024 Egaeus Press anthology *Infernal Mysteries*, and another is due in the October folk-horror anthology *Harvest the Night* (Chthonic Matter). She works at a used bookstore in a stunningly gorgeous town in the ass-end of Oregon.

Sarah R New has been writing since she was 6. She specialises primarily in horror or fiction with horrific elements, but also writes speculative fiction and non-fiction. Her self-published travel memoir, *The Great European Escape*, was released in 2023, and her Gothic horror novella, *Amissis Liberis*, was published in 2024. Sarah lives in the UK but frequently travels internationally. She can be found on Bluesky, Instagram and Twitter under the username aldbera, or at sarahrnew.wordpress.com.

Marcelle Perks has an MA in Media Studies and has worked for the British Film Institute and film/TV magazine publisher Visual Imagination. She has written for a range of film publications, including *Alternative Europe: Eurotrash and British Exploitation Cinema*, *The Goth Bible*, *The BFI Companion to Horror*, *British Horror Cinema*, *Gay Times*, *Fangoria*, *The Dark Side*, *Videoworld*, *Shivers*, *Flesh and Blood*, *Diabolik*, and *Kamera*. She is the author of non-fiction books, short fiction, and her debut novel *Night Driver* was published in 2018. In the German film *Warte warte nur ein weilchen* (2020) she gets killed at her own book launch!

Books and stories have played major roles in **Alex Ringer**'s life since before he can remember, when he would turn pages for his parents and grandparents as they read to him, and repeat the lines of the 'Mr Men' books despite being unable to read them. They have been ever present in his upbringing in the literature-rich city of his birth, Oxford, providing escapism at every turn. They are a passion he have been lucky to foster with the tutelage of the amazing English department at Loughborough University, and will pursue further at master's level in the coming academic year.

Frank Schildiner is a martial arts instructor at Amorosi's Martial Arts in New Jersey. He is the writer of the novels, *Caesar Now Be Still*, *Napoleon's Vampire Hunters*, *The Last Days of Atlantis*, *Secrets of the Nine*, two issues of the *MX Book of New Sherlock Holmes Stories*, *Hidden Horrors* as well as several short stories and articles on various subjects. He resides in New Jersey with two cats who are indifferent to his work.

Ashley Stokes is the author of *Gigantic* (Unsung Stories) and *The Syllabus of Errors* (Unthank Books). His recent short fiction includes pieces in *Interzone*, *Great British Horror 9* (Black Shuck Books), *Chthonic Matter*, *For Tomorrow* (Black Shuck Books), *Devour*, *Dark Lane Digest*, *Three-Lobed Burning Eye*, *I-Z Digital*, *Weird Horror*, *Phantasmagoria*, *At the Lighthouse* (Eibonvale Press), *Cloister Fox*, *Black Static*, *Nightscript*, *The Ghastling*, *Out of the Darkness* (Unsung Stories) and more. He lives in the East of England where he's a ghost and ghostwriter.

Pete W Sutton is a writer and editor. His two short story collections – *A Tiding of Magpies* and *The Museum for Forgetting* – were shortlisted for Best Collection in the British Fantasy Awards in 2017 & 2022 respectively. His novel – *Seven Deadly Swords* – was published by Grimbold Books. He has edited several short story anthologies and is the editor for the British Fantasy Society *Horizons* fiction magazine. www.petewsutton.com

Currently studying Latin, Ancient Greek, and Ancient Classical History at Newcastle University (because his obsessive love of Doctor Who and horror films wasn't nerdy enough), **Benjamin Kurt Unsworth** writes short stories and reviews/essays for various outlets, drinks copious cups of tea, loves knitting, and buys far too many waistcoats and velvet jackets.

Last year, **Darcy L Wood** attended the prestigious Clarion Workshop in San Diego. Apart from being a reader for *Skull & Laurel*, as well as the editor of a local heritage railway magazine, Darcy lives with a Swedish beau in deepest darkest Oxfordshire. Despite being a big wimp when it comes to horror films, she still loves a good scare. Celtic and Slavic blood thrums in her veins. Darcy's latest short fiction appeared in *Amazing Stories*, *Cosmorama* and *Creepy Podcast*.

Sophie Essex has edited six previous anthologies including *Dreamland* (Black Shuck Books) and *At The Lighthouse* (Eibonvale Press), both of which were shortlisted for British Fantasy Society awards. Her publishing company, Salò Press, focusses on poetry and prose chapbooks in a variety of genres. You can find her online @capitanofelixio

www.ingramcontent.com/pod-product-compliance
Lightning Source LLC
Chambersburg PA
CBHW030323080526
44584CB00012B/686